HIDDEN INVESTING

WHAT THE WEALTHIEST 1% KNOW THAT WE DON'T...

HOLLY WILLIAMS

Copyright © 2020

Beverly Hills Publishing

All Rights Reserved

ISBN: 9798-649-12-2498

The information and descriptions presented in this book and in the Hidden Investing newsletters and website are intended for adults, age 18 and over, and are solely for informational and educational purposes. Holly Williams does not give legal, psychological, or financial advice. Before beginning any new business or personal development routine, or if you have specific legal, psychological, or medical concerns, a medical, financial, legal, or other professional should be consulted.

Any reproduction, republication, or other distribution of this work, including, without limitation, the duplication, copying, scanning, uploading, and making available via the internet or any other means, without the express permission of the publisher is illegal and punishable by law, and the knowing acquisition of an unauthorized reproduction of this work may subject the acquirer to liability. Please purchase only authorized electronic or print editions of this work and do not participate in or encourage electronic piracy of copyrighted materials. Your support of the author's rights is appreciated.

This document is geared towards providing exact and reliable information with regards to the topic and issue covered. The publication is sold with the idea that the publisher is not required to render accounting, officially permitted, or otherwise, qualified services. If advice is necessary, legal or professional, a practiced individual in the profession should be ordered.

From a Declaration of Principles which was accepted and approved equally by a Committee of the American Bar Association and a Committee of Publishers and Associations.

In no way is it legal to reproduce, duplicate, or transmit any part of this document in either electronic means or in printed format. Recording of this publication is strictly prohibited and any storage of this document is not allowed unless with written permission from the publisher. All rights reserved.

The information provided herein is stated to be truthful and consistent, in that any liability, in terms of inattention or otherwise, by any usage or abuse of any policies, processes, or directions contained within is the solitary and utter responsibility of the recipient reader. Under no circumstances will any legal responsibility or blame be held against the publisher for any reparation, damages, or monetary loss due to the information herein, either directly or indirectly. Respective authors own all copyrights not held by the publisher. The information herein is offered for informational purposes solely, and is universal as so. The presentation of the information is without contract or any type of guarantee assurance.

The trademarks that are used are without any consent, and the publication of the trademark is without permission or backing by the trademark owner. All trademarks and brands within this book are for clarifying purposes only and are the owned by the owners themselves, not affiliated with this document.

©2020 and beyond, Beverly Hills Publishing. All Rights Reserved.

Contents

DEDICATION — 6
APPRECIATION — 7
FOREWARD — 8
What the Top One Percent Know That We Don't — 12

Myth #1
The Higher Your Income, The Richer You Are — 22

Myth #2
The Rich Are Greedy – They Get Richer While The Rest Of Us Struggle — 33

Myth #3
The Tax Code Is Designed To Tell Us How Much Tax We Need To Pay — 44

Myth #4
Manage Your Wealth And Leave A Legacy By Diversifying Your Investments — 55

Myth #5
Your 401K Will Grow Tax-Free And Provide You With A Wonderful Retirement — 68

Myth #6
Put Your Money In No Load Funds And Avoid High Fees — 82

Myth #7
Trust The Experts — 93

Myth #8
Hire A Financial Advisor To Plan Your Retirement — 102

Myth #9
Real Estate Investing Is Risky And Unpredictable — 111

Myth #10
The Good Deals In Real Estate Are All Gone — 118

Conclusion — 129

DEDICATION

To Investors everywhere that are searching for a better way. This is our time. www.KeepMore.com

APPRECIATION

Thanks to all to my amazing investors, partners, and family for trusting, believing, and joining me on this journey. Thanks to Joe Fairless and Trevor McGregor for showing me the way. And thanks to Andréa Albright and the team at Beverly Hills Publishing for helping me put it all together.

FOREWARD

There's something about money and investing that we all think we understand, but in the end, most of us do not. In fact, as a Master Coach and Business Strategist, I've dedicated over 25,000 hours to working with entrepreneurs, business owners and people from all walks of life, in order to help them to understand how to make money, achieve success and create a phenomenal quality of life for themselves and their families. Doing this work has given me an incredible perspective on how "average people" think, behave, and ultimately struggle when it comes to investing money and getting it to grow. I've also been able to see how the top 1% think and behave much differently when it comes to investing their money, as they somehow seem to have the "competitive edge" or know things that average people do not, in terms of how to use that money to achieve extraordinary investing results.

In speaking with many clients about this time and time again, one client of mine in particular caught my attention one day, when she was able to articulate the difference between the two so eloquently and with amazing clarity and precision. In fact, I was blown away at how she was able to put it into "simple terms" and describe it in a way that if explained to anyone, would help them to understand it. That client was none other than the amazing author of this book: Holly Williams.

As I started working with Holly back in 2017, I knew there was something special about her. She'd always come to the call with incredible energy and with so many things to talk about, including business, money, investing or real estate (or sometimes about her amazing daughter and husband). As I got to know Holly really well, I truly enjoyed working with her and admired her as she had achieved a phenomenal level of success in her corporate advertising career, with her family, AND with her investments as well.

With that said, and in listening to her entire story, it certainly didn't start that way. She would tell me how she had originally tried using traditional investments to grow her net worth but soon came to realize that there was a disadvantage to doing it the way we're all told to do it, and that it limited her opportunities for massive growth AND forced her to pay more in taxes.

In thinking that there had to be a better way, Holly set off on a quest to discover how the wealthiest among us invest. She knew that real estate was one way to defer taxes and build generational wealth, but she discovered that the wealthy had access to invest passively in large income-producing commercial projects as an equity member. As she immersed herself into this world, found opportunities, and began to invest like the 1%, her life began to change.

Holly soon made it her MISSION to learn everything she could and network with the top entrepreneurs in the industry. As she began sharing what she learned with her friends and advertising colleagues, she was shocked to learn that most people, smart people, professional people, didn't know about these types of investments, known as real estate syndications. Holly would try to show them how it all worked and realized that not just herself, but most of us are programmed to invest in real estate either via publicly-traded REITs and help Wall Street get richer or to take on the risk and responsibility of buying rental property on their own. Holly knew that 1% had been taking advantage of real estate syndications and many other private investments for generations, but people who hadn't grown up wealthy simply weren't in the club. As more of her friends began to open their minds and take action however, their lives began to change too.

She finally reached the threshold where she knew it was her mission to educate and inform people to the massive advantages as to why investing passively in real estate was so powerful, and why it was her number one choice for wealth creation.

In the pages of this book, not only will you learn what those strategies are, but Holly pulls back the curtain and reveals what most people don't want you to know about traditional investing. Not only will you get some incredible new perspectives on what truly goes on behind the scenes with the stock market, mutual funds, and 401K's, but you'll quickly see how the average person has been taught to systematically follow the herd and do what the masses are programmed to do.

In summary, if you want to be successful and invest your money to create an abundance of wealth for you, for your family and for generations to come, you owe it to yourself to read this book cover to cover. Not only will you get everything explained in simple terms, but you'll be able to take immediate action to follow in the footsteps that Holly and I both know will support your ultimate financial outcomes for your life and generations to come.

Sincerely,

Trevor McGregor

Master Platinum Coach and Business Strategist

(aka Holly's Coach)

INTRODUCTION:
What the Top One Percent Know That We Don't

Our belief systems run deep. They are ingrained and reinforced in us from a young age through our families, our schools, and the barrage of media influence that surrounds us every day. By the time we reach adulthood, much of our view of the world has been shaped for us, and that view becomes the navigational map that guides our decision-making into adulthood. Of all the ideas influenced by this map, perhaps the most damaging is the way we think about money. From how we make it, to how we save, spend, and invest: all of it is all driven by those hard-wired beliefs. Those beliefs are difficult—sometimes impossible—to rewire.

I was no different. I tried to follow that map to the letter.

I spent my early years absorbing everything I was taught. I went to school, got a job, focused on building my 401K, and lived below my means. I was taught to invest in the stock market, and to diversify my assets between stocks, bonds, and later on, insurance and annuities. I was told to buy the biggest house that I could afford, and that it would be my greatest asset moving forward. I was taught all of these things, and told they were the smartest ways to ensure financial security.

What I know now is that only some of that is true. There is more to the story. I wasn't taught the rest, and likely neither were you.

I went along, adhering to what I had learned from my parents, my school, and my immediate network of friends and family. Out of college I hired a financial advisor, maxed out the 401K, and when I moved to New York, I bought a Manhattan apartment as soon as I possibly could.

Sometime in the late 1990's I read a book by Robert Kyosaki, entitled *Rich Dad, Poor Dad*. It focused heavily on real estate, and the ideas made a lot of sense to me. But, my hard-wired view of the world told me that it was probably too good to be true and that Kyosaki was ultimately just trying to sell books. I stuck to my beliefs. However, that book did get me thinking, and it provided me with my first glimpse into another world. The world of the wealthiest Americans.

I was inspired, and a little research led me to begin looking at investment properties in my hometown of Houston. I found some early success, but it was a lot of work to look for properties, evaluate them, and manage them remotely. The fact that I was living 1,500 miles away further complicated things. I already had a career, and between the voices of my parents, personal finance magazines, and now with the Internet and cable, I was being told every single day that the smart, financially-sound decision was investing in the stock market, working hard, and moving up the corporate ladder.

I did move up the ladder. I tell people that I crawled and scratched my way to the middle! I was having a great time in New York. Over the years I met a fantastic man who owned a 4-family house in Brooklyn that needed a LOT of work. We had a wonderful daughter. Life became busy fairly quickly.

From where I started, and with a little luck along the way, I was able to build a pretty fantastic life. A life that I'm so very grateful for to this day. We renovated that 4-family home, our daughter is healthy and thriving, and after 19 years I am still happily married.

Despite my success, around nine years ago my fundamental beliefs began to shift. This period of my life was one of great transformation.

During that time, I found myself paying nearly 50 percent of my earnings in taxes. It seemed absurd to be losing so much of my hard-earned wealth, but when I complained to anyone, I felt guilty. After all, I was making a good living. But I saw more and more of my prosperity disappear to the Federal Government, the state of New York, and, to add insult to injury, there was New York City income tax on top of both. Then, two things happened that led to my ultimate financial awakening.

The Changes that Made All the Difference

The first wake-up call was a glimpse at my future, as I watched my parents' retirement savings slowly evaporate over their final years. When the stock market collapsed, they still needed income and had to continue to withdraw their investments, even when the market was down, to pay the bills. I saw the carnage firsthand, as they were forced to pay full income tax on that money, most of which was technically capital gains, but because it was withdrawn from a 401K it was taxed as 100% regular income. All they had worked for began to quickly erode.

Of course, they had invested in "safe" bonds and some stock mutual funds, but no matter how conservative their savings were, things still went south. Those ALL went down in 2008, but my parents were still counting on those 401Ks for income. When they got sick and needed help, things went from bad to worse. No matter how safe they thought they were, they were forced to pull their money and then pay taxes. And so, between the whims of Wall Street and the Federal Government, their financial picture in the last years of their lives was not the one that their advisors had painted for them years before. I watched much of the wealth they had built disappear. It was shocking to see people who seemed to do everything right begin to struggle and worry. There had to be a better way.

The second jolt came a couple of years later when I received a 1099 from my broker telling me I had earned $65,000. Like many people, my financial advisor had invested some of my money across several mutual funds, and some of them were outside of my IRA. We've all seen those 1099s that tell us that we've made $5,000-$10,000. I would get them every January and think, "Wow, aren't I doing great?" I would pass them along to my accountant, (who I know now was simply a tax preparer), and not think about it again.

After that 1099 told me that I had "made" $65,000, and a couple of others showed some "profits" as well, I was shocked when I was told at tax time that I owed around $25,000 of that money in capital gains taxes. I hadn't even withdrawn any of the capital, and I still had to pay taxes on money that I didn't have!

That's when I realized that, within those funds, the fund manager is buying and selling. When they do that, as long as there is a net gain, YOU pay capital gains on that money even if you never take it out. In addition, the costs of those trades are almost always taken out of your returns. The fund managers, and their companies that spend billions of dollars in advertising every year, buy, sell, and earn net gains that WE pay capital gains tax on. We as the customer pay for all of it, in addition to any other hidden expenses that emerge.

I realized that not only was I paying taxes on roughly 50% of my salary, but I also owed another $25,000 in taxes on money that was still only on paper. Money that could very well lose value in the future! When I internalized the 1099 that told me I had "made" $65,000 really meant that I owed $25,000 in taxes, I woke up. I realized right then and there that taxes were far and away my biggest expense and had the smallest return. I remembered what Robert Kyosaki had told me years before, and I began to search in earnest for a better way.

An Alternative Appears

My solution came in the form of a good friend from Texas. He was also interested in real estate, and I got a call from him about an apartment complex he had discovered. He was looking for investors to buy it with him, and he told me that he was going to manage it and get "limited partners" like myself to buy it, and that we would all get the benefits of real estate investing but he would do all of the work.

I invested with him, and that's when I began to learn about the world of multifamily syndication and how the 1% invest their money. I understood apartments because I had certainly lived in many of them over the years, but I'd never heard of passively investing in them.

When the checks started coming, and I realized that I was making income without selling the asset, that the asset kept adding value, and that I was able to defer taxes on that income, I was amazed. I thought that I was the only one that didn't know about this! I began asking my friends who were much wealthier than me, and they had no idea what I was talking about either.

Several months later, my Texas friend found a second apartment complex in Houston and asked me if I could help him evaluate it, raise the funds to buy it, and join him as a General Partner in the project.

I started by calling my friends and family to present what I knew was an amazing opportunity that most of us don't have access to, and that's when I found out that they all had the same basic wiring as I did. They, too, were deeply ingrained with the standard ideas of wealth and investing.

My friends thought it was super risky, too good to be true, and possibly illegal. Some were afraid that they wouldn't have control over the investment. I was honestly shocked, and right then and there I realized how misleading the roadmap that most of us are provided is.

You see, the wealthiest people in our country have access to opportunities that most of us don't. A few of my friends invested because they trusted me, but the rest were simply too wary. They'd never heard of an investment like this before. Some of them asked their financial advisors and even they didn't know, so they told them that the deal was risky, too good to be true, and quite possibly illegal.

I've come to realize that multifamily syndications, if done properly, are none of those things. The more risks that you can mitigate, the more control you have, and that the 1 percent has been investing in multifamily syndications for generations. It's one of many private, hidden investments that are not publicly available. Hidden investments like multifamily syndication can be, in my personal experience, safer and often more lucrative. The biggest difference is they are not available to the public and cannot be advertised freely.

The only way to invest in private syndication is to have a relationship with one or more of the general partners. I had offered my friends and family the same opportunity that my friend had offered me, and they had raised all of the same concerns that I had. It was something that they had never heard of and didn't understand. Not because it's complicated—in fact, it's very simple, but because they'd been programmed to think a certain way about investing—just as I was.

This book aims to shift your thinking in two dramatic ways. To transform your approach to investing, you must first rewire decades of misleading financial information. I'm going to highlight ten common investing beliefs that I know today are simply myths, and explain the reality, based on my personal experiences, of the hidden financial world.

In doing so, I also aim to show how and exactly why many of these hidden investments are most often consistent, secure, and profitable. We are going to dive into the numbers from my personal investments, and I'll share how consistent revenue streams from investments that most of us don't know are even an option, are indeed possible.

What the wealthiest 1 percent know that we don't.

First, a disclaimer. This is only one book, and multifamily syndication is only one hidden investment. However, it's what I learned about first, and it is what I believe, at least for me and probably many of you, to be the best investment out there for conservative, passive income. Over the years I've become obsessed with multifamily syndications, and how the 1% have invested in them for years to provide secure and steady income. I'm 58 years old, I retired in 2018 last year on that income, and this is what I've learned.

CHAPTER 1:

Myth #1

The Higher Your Income, The Richer You Are

Reality: The Uber - Wealthy Are Hard-Wired to Think Differently About Money

Before I felt comfortable investing like the 1%, I had to dramatically change how I think about money and my finances. I had to rewire years of bad information. Most of the Ultra-Wealthy have a completely different relationship with money compared to those of us who are merely successful. When I finished college, all I learned was to negotiate the highest salary I could. The 1% look at money as something that works for them, not something that they work for. The 1% think about building wealth, as opposed to working for W-2 income that is taxed at the highest rates possible. They're not counting on a job to provide 100% of their income and savings, because they have income-generating investments.

You see, there's a huge difference between income and wealth. Wealth is not how much money is in your bank account. Wealth is about assets. Assets that build wealth are assets that pay you while the value of the asset grows. Investments like this can provide generational income because they don't go away. In fact, they grow in value over time. Most of us call that passive income, but I believe that there is no such thing as passive income, because the money has to come from somewhere. The beauty of multifamily syndication, though, is that I was able to continue to excel in my career, while I built generational wealth in real estate without having to do the work!

When you invest in assets that build wealth, when you do need the income it flows from your wealth as opposed to selling a stock. The wealth is still there. The wealthy don't spend their money, they invest it! The way to build generational wealth and avoid what happened to my parents is to invest your money in cash-flowing assets as often as you can, and cash-flowing assets are what most of the truly wealthy use as a source of income. Especially for retirement.

Contrast that to stocks and the other public, institutional investments that most of us are taught to invest heavily in. With most of those, they either return very little, or you have completely sell the asset to see your income. Especially with stocks, it's gone forever. Think about that...it's gone. You have to sell the golden goose to get the egg!

Then, to add insult to injury, it's typically taxed on top of those fees. The uber-wealthy don't look at an investment as an expense or a cost. They look at an investment as, "This is actually going to save me time and money by working for me, and most likely lower my tax bill to boot." They look for assets that continue to grow, all the while providing income. My parents wanted nothing more than to leave me and my brother with a nice inheritance. I now know what a huge difference thinking about wealth versus income can make.

> *The wealthy think of money logically. The rest of us are too emotional with our money.*

Instead of using money as a tool, we worry about it, we use it to boost our confidence, and we feel fantastic or we feel terrible depending upon whether we have it or not. Amazingly, successful people that are otherwise highly competent can turn into shriveling, scared, scarcity-driven bundles of emotion when money is involved. We will talk in the next chapter about an abundance mentality vs a scarcity mentality, but a scarcity mentality is how society has programmed most of us to think. That is why the stock market is largely driven by emotion, and not logic. If it was logical, it would go up when a company was making more money and it would go down when a company was underperforming.

It should be simple, but a company can literally have the greatest year ever and their stock will be at historic lows, and a company that makes no income at all can have a soaring stock price. Some of this we can justify logically because of market conditions, management changes, or new strategies on the horizon, but most of the time, who knows? The professionals tell us that they don't know either, and every day successful business executives all over the country freely hand over their life savings to people that readily tell us that they don't know what is going to happen, but that "It will be ok in the long run." How logical is that really? Think about it.

When I invest in an apartment complex, quite literally 100 percent of the time, if the operating income of the asset goes up, I make more money. When the operating income of the asset goes down, I make less money. I can tell you exactly what I'm doing to mitigate risk, and I can tell you exactly how that asset has performed in a myriad of market conditions. People move in, they pay the rent, we collect the rent and pay the expenses, and the rest is profit. It's totally logical, yet some of the smartest people I know tell me that they know about stocks, but don't understand real estate. I scratch my head because the 1% knows this and invests based upon logic.

> The uber-wealthy design their life, and then they plan for enough money to support that life.

Money is simply a tool to get to where they want to go. What makes me really happy? What kind of life do I want to have? Do I want to be in a big city? Do I want to be in a small town? The wealthy have lofty goals, and they never lose sight of them. People equipped with a wealth mindset decide what they want from life first, and then they design their cash flow accordingly. The rich make a plan to be rich, and they execute that plan.

Like many of us, I moved to NYC for a job, not even thinking about whether or not I wanted to live there. I moved to NY because it was where the opportunity was to make the most money. Now, I love NY, and I'm happy to be here, but I was certainly willing to sacrifice my quality of life just to make money.

The wealthy think about money as a tool to get to where they need to go. It's not the end game. The wealthy certainly want and need to make money, but they invest in things such as real estate syndications, businesses, and even oil wells. And most of the very best investment opportunities in those asset classes are hidden from people like us.

When I discovered that I could invest passively in real estate, I began to see those opportunities and the possibilities. When we buy a multi-family apartment complex, of which there are thousands, and thousands, and thousands across the country, we buy them from REITs, we buy them from hedge funds, we buy them from family offices, and we buy them from other entrepreneurs. We also invest right along with our investors, and since we count on the income the asset generates to live, we're incentivized to make that cash flow. It's called alignment of interests, and we will get into that later, but it's something that the stock market and most other public investments simply don't have. When I get richer, all of the people I am working with get richer. When the tide comes, it raises all boats.

The 1 percent understand this. They also understand that the costs of stocks and mutual funds, the tax implications, and that interests of everyone involved are not necessarily aligned. You see, most financial advisors get paid whether or not we make money. Many are not as wealthy as we are, and often they do not invest in the same products that they recommend to us. Now, I realize that I'm making a few blanket statements and that not all financial advisors are the same. However, those are definitely questions that you should ask before you invest with anyone.

> *The wealthy have a different view of what is risky and what isn't.*

Most of the 1% look at their investments in the stock market as risky, simply because most of them are. If I buy a stock, I have little insight into that company or its internal workings.

For instance, I don't truly know the various market risks of Apple when I buy their stock. I don't know how a new trade agreement might impact their business. I've made money with Apple stock, but at the end of the day, I have an iPhone—I like it—and that's about what I know. Most financial advisors will tell you that they don't know, either.

The stock market is not a bad thing. Financial advisors are not bad people. It's just that most of them don't know about hidden investments either. They go to business school, but they don't teach about hidden investments in colleges and business schools because the professors don't know. Then, after college, they may get a job on Wall Street, and whatever company they join typically has a training program, and that company trains them on what they want them to know. That company has hired them to help them sell their products and generate transactions that make money for the firm. Most financial advisers are incentivized to offer their clients only those products that their boss wants them to sell. Even if they wanted, they are usually limited in what they have access to.

You should also know that things become very, very different once you reach a net worth of $20M+. The wealthy often have access to invest directly into businesses, bypassing all of the fees that Wall Street must charge to cover the costs of their offices and high salaries. That kind of wealth can get you teams of CPAs and access to private accounts with large banks and funds who take companies public, enabling early access to investments before the general public. That kind of net worth is also what it used to take to get into the kind of multifamily syndication investments that I was able to retire on. Those opportunities are still largely hidden from the rest of us.

The truth is that all investors are not created equal, and the wealthy enjoy access to many things that we don't. I very much doubt that Warren Buffett, Bill Gates, Jeff Bezos, and a good many of the wealthiest people in our country are logging into their brokerage accounts and buying stocks like so many of us are. If they do have a regular brokerage account, I will bet that major sources of their wealth are in investments that the rest of us would believe were especially risky and/or too good to be true.

The wealthiest people in America have been investing in private opportunities for decades, but they have mostly done it through high net-worth private funds, many of which require a net worth of $20-$30 million to participate. No wonder most of us don't know about them!

There is another hurdle in place for those of us who didn't grow up wealthy. A majority of private investments are only available to those whose income and/or net worth is high enough. Being an accredited investor is required. The SEC, Securities and Exchange Commission, created the accredited investor designation to help prevent investors from being taken advantage of in the private markets. If you make over $200,000 a year and/or have a total net worth of $1 million, you are likely an accredited investor. For the most part, you can "self-certify" but to participate in many private investments, including many real estate syndications, you must be an accredited investor. The SEC web site goes into great detail about what it means to be an accredited investor, and I urge you to go there and learn more. What amazes me though is the number of people that honestly don't know what an accredited investor is. I was an accredited investor before I even knew what it was. If you are reading this book there is a good chance that you are as well, and may not even know it.

Some syndications can take a few "sophisticated investors", but unless you are accredited or sophisticated, you typically can't participate but it depends on how the sponsor sets up the project and registers things with the SEC. As a matter of fact, depending on how that structure works, some syndication partners are even prohibited from discussing the deal with you unless you are an accredited investor!

So an unintended consequence of this regulation is that, even though it's set up to protect people, it can make it even more difficult to find really good hidden investments.

This definitely explains why you might not have ever heard of real estate syndications and other private investments. However, most of the one percent are well-aware of their accredited investor status, they surround themselves with experts who have a vast knowledge of our tax code, and they take full advantage of both.

The last six years have been as much about unlearning what I thought I knew about investing as they have been learning about new opportunities. I've come to believe that our government truly doesn't know what is best for us and that Wall Street isn't far behind. I've learned that financial products that we are told have "no fees" still carry tremendous expenses that need to be paid for and that it's almost always our returns that foot the bill. I'm also convinced that many of the top "experts" are simply not. Much of what I was taught about money and investing, along with my attitudes about wealth and the wealthy, were simply myths.

In talking with investors, knowing how foreign investments outside of wall street sounded to me, and how suspicious and afraid I was about multifamily syndications in the beginning, I realize now that most of those fears are rooted in the view of the world that we're given. But just because something is given to me doesn't mean that I have to keep it.

Today, I think of wealth much more than I think about income, and I honestly try to have the LOWEST income possible. I think of my investments in real estate syndications and other private investments as my "safe" investments, and the stock market is where my riskiest investments sit. This new approach was a 180-degree flip from where I was ten years ago. And I have never been happier and more successful.

CHAPTER 2:

Myth #2

The Rich Are Greedy – They Get Richer While The Rest Of Us Struggle

Reality: When the Rich Get Richer, They Aren't Taking It From the Rest of Us

We highlighted in the previous chapter how the one percent simply think about money differently. At the root of that thinking is a mindset that permeates through every aspect of the lives of a majority of the Uber-Wealthy. From how they approach investments, to what they choose to spend their time on. In short, most of the wealthiest people in America look and think about life differently than most of us.

We regularly hear about wealthy people who, for whatever reason, lose everything, and five years later they've made it back in spades. Conversely, everyone has heard about the lottery winners, star athletes, and everyday people come into life-changing money all of a sudden, and then 5 years later they are broke. Why is that?

It's not that the rich are better people or deserve more, it comes down to mindset. At the root of that thinking is a mindset of abundance as opposed to scarcity.

People with a scarcity mentality are always living in fear that they're going to lose out, instead of looking for opportunities that are often right in front of them.

As I write this, there is a large group of powerful people in this country that are very loudly telling everyone who will listen that being in the top 1% is bad, that rich people are bad, that being a landlord is bad. There is a lot of talk about instituting a wealth tax, how the rich are getting richer at the expense of everyone else, and how we should redistribute that wealth. That has never worked and will never work, largely because of the mindset that most of the 1% are equipped with.

You see, the rich have a mindset of abundance in all areas of their lives, and that naturally translates into more money. It sounds crazy, but it's so true and I've seen it firsthand in my life. I've never wished bad things on anyone, and I was never particularly jealous or, god-forbid, sabotaged anyone's career. But I spent most of my career believing that if someone else got promoted over me, then my time was essentially over at any company that I worked for. That there was only room for one superstar. That there was a finite amount of money, and if others got more, then I would get less. In actuality, there is an infinite amount of abundance out there, as long as we set clear goals and reach out and grab it. There are opportunities everywhere to make money. If you change your mindset, you're much more open to those opportunities.

I left my office job in 2018, and since then I've made twice as much as I was making when I was working for someone else. I pay half of the taxes that I used to. I'm the same person. I'm no more talented than I was two years ago so what changed? My attitude did. As did my mindset.

People with an abundance mentality believe that ultimately the universe is on the side of good, it wants us to succeed, and that opportunities for growth are limitless. Scarcity mentalities are rooted in fear. Fear that there won't be enough, fear that we aren't good enough, aren't smart enough, too fat, too skinny, too poor, and generally just not enough. It takes courage to logically determine how real those fears are, and walk through them towards abundance. Courage is simply fear with faith, and developing an abundance mentality begins with faith.

If you want to have faith in abundance, just look around. All over America businesses sprout out of seemingly nowhere and grow to be worth millions and millions of dollars. We see our economy expand and it never stops. Yes, it may temporarily slow down, but it always expands in the end. When I go home to Houston, I hardly recognize the place. There are freeways and toll roads that weren't there when I lived there, and entire neighborhoods in places that used to be cow pastures. This happens more quickly than you'd expect. It's a universal truth that society expands, and we are constantly amazed at how cities and towns grow around us. There is ALWAYS more.

If you ask, the universe will reward you. I've seen it happen in my own life, I've seen it happen in the lives of others, and it can happen to you. The problem is that most of us let the universe control our destiny as opposed to determining where we want to be and then going there. There is more than enough, but I've learned from the rich that there are some steps to take before this shift occurs. Remember, I began my hidden investing journey in 2013, and it took me until 2018 to leave my W-2 job. It doesn't have to take you that long, but there are definitely some things that the rich just believe. When I realized that they were right, I began to see more and more abundance out there. The reasons that the rich are rich and possess this overall abundance mindset stems from the way they think about their lives and approach the idea of wealth.

The Wealthy Don't See Themselves as Victims

Many things in life are simply unfair. Some of us are born into great wealth, while others struggle to pay rent every month. Some people are born with physical disabilites, some with mental disabilities, and some people just have a raw deal all the way around. But the fact is, we are all victims of something, and it's easy to latch on to this victim mindset because many things in life may not go your way. Our society loves victims, gives them lots of attention, and we do everything that we can to compensate them for their victimhood. We absolutely love victims in this country. We love to talk about how rough people have it because it makes a good news story.

But when we begin to see ourselves as victims, we are stuck. When we look at others and think how much "luckier" they are than us, and look how hard I have it, we can never see the full picture. The truth is that nothing is ever truly as it seems. As good or as bad.

Have you ever watched a really good skier going down a mountain? They look so relaxed like they are just gliding down on the skis, letting gravity take over. But if you are a skier, you know that skiing is one of the most aggressive sports out there. You have to take on the mountain and conquer it! It's about leaning forward and shifting your weight to create momentum as well as control. If you aren't aggressive, if you just sit back and count on gravity to get you to the bottom of the mountain, you will fall, and depending on the size of the mountain and your speed, you could fall badly. This helps illustrate the idea that nothing is ever as it seems. What we see is not the whole story. We don't see what is happening in the background. That skier worked extremely hard to get to the point that their skiing could appear effortless.

I have a good friend named Joe Fairless. Joe is a multi-family syndicator and coach, and we met many years ago through an advisory board that we are both a part of. Joe has been incredibly successful over the past several years buying apartments, writing books, and teaching others to buy apartments. I often meet people who think that things have happened very quickly for Joe, and if you are one of those people you should come and talk to me. I remember Joe before he wrote four books and accumulated a $500M apartment portfolio. When we would travel to look at properties together, I used to pick him up at fleabag motels where I was honestly afraid while sitting in the parking lot waiting for him to come out to the car.

I've seen Joe during the high points and the low ones, and he will be the first to tell you that working long hours on a long road got him to where he is today. He learned, he applied what he learned, he had help along the way, and most of all, he helped others along the way.

Now he's one of the top multifamily syndicators in the business. He has a beautiful family, a successful company, he's in demand as a speaker, and has one of the highest-ranked real estate podcasts in the country. He seems to have it all, but I'm sure that he still has problems and challenges today, but they are just different than they were back then. Nothing is ever as it seems, and continuous growth doesn't happen without challenges and uncomfortable situations. Whatever impressions you have of others or if you look objectively at your situation, I can guarantee you that you aren't seeing the complete story from all sides.

The rich know that things are never as bad, or as good as they seem, and when something bad happens to them, they do their best to move out of anything that resembles a victim mentality as soon as possible. Sure, they may get down after a loss for five minutes, five days, or, if it's a really bad loss, five weeks or years, but they know that the only way to move forward is to stop thinking about what a victim they are. How? By focusing on a thing called gratitude.

The Wealthy are Grateful

Everyone has people, particular skills, or relevant experience in their lives that can help them solve problems, as well as see and take advantage of opportunities. Joe Fairless calls them assets. In his book, *Best Ever Apartment Syndication Book,* one of the first things that Joe talks about is how to identify the assets that you have at your disposal. Different situations call for different assets.

Every single one of us has assets, but at least for me, I have trouble seeing them if I'm not grateful. It's really about being grateful, knowing, and understanding the assets that you have at your disposal and then making the best use of them. When I get stuck these days, the first thing that I do is start a gratitude list of all of the things that I'm grateful for at that moment. Almost immediately, my brain starts to think of resources that I have to get out of whatever mess I happen to be in.

Identifying the right asset for a particular problem is key. For instance, I married a wonderful man. I could write an entire book just about how great my husband is, but I can guarantee you that he won't be the first person to read *this* book. He's going to tell everyone he knows that they should read it, how successful I am, and all about the apartments I invest in. But what my husband won't do is tell *me* how great the book is, and how awesome I am. He may read this eventually, or he may not, and that used to really upset me. I would feel unappreciated, unloved, and angry. After all, what a jerk, right? Who doesn't rush to read his wife's book even as she's writing it? But for some reason, he's simply just not a guy that is interested in where I work, how much money I make, what I'm doing at work, what I'm writing or what I'm not writing. I know that he's proud of me, though, because I hear him talking to his friends about me, expressing his amazement about how fabulous I am. He just doesn't tell ME those things, and expecting him to inspire confidence and enthusiasm for my work would be counterproductive.

If I want encouragement relative to real estate investing or writing, I have other people in my life that I can turn to. My coach, Trevor McGregor, my friends, and extended family. As a matter of fact, all I really have to do is post any minor accomplishment on Facebook, and tons of people tell me how great I am! It always feels nice to have that support, and I'm confident that no matter what life throws my way, that I will find the assets to get through it. Make a list of the people and things in your life that you are grateful for and why you are grateful, and watch your mindset begin to change.

The Wealthy Understand the True Value of Time

Time is the great equalizer. We all have exactly the same amount of time in a day, and the wealthy are particularly good at making the most of their 24-hour allotment. They know how much their time is worth, and spend their time on high-value activities. My high-value activities include spending time with my investors and business partners, visiting and analyzing properties, reading and learning, speaking and attending conferences, working with my coaches and mentors, and the most important of all – spending time with my family and others that I love. Things that aren't high-value I try very hard to outsource, or at least spend as little time as possible on them. Never waste your own time. (Or anyone else's if you can help it.)

The 1% Know Their Value

In our country, most of us earn money based on the value that we create. The wealthy know what their time is worth, and they charge accordingly. If someone wants to pay them less than their value, they don't take the job. Period.

The 1% also invest in learning to increase their value. My investing journey exploded when I began working with my business coach, Trevor McGregor. All top athletes have coaches, and now I realize that most successful executives do too. I thought it was expensive at first, but it has paid off in spades. (After reading this Trevor will probably raise your rates!)

I also participate in several mastermind groups to learn and be inspired by others who are more successful. Often, these people are experts in other areas outside of multifamily real estate. Proximity is power, and being with people that are far more successful than I am forces me to up my game to keep up. I also belong to two book clubs, one focused on real estate, and one focused on general business books. I've learned from them and have met new business partners as well.

I can almost guarantee that if you stop thinking like a victim, take an inventory of the assets that you have around you, practice being grateful every day, and focus on those activities that are high value, you will begin to internalize and realize the power of the abundance mindset. This mindset unlocks the rest of the secret to success. Guaranteed or your money back.

CHAPTER 3:

Myth #3

The Tax Code Is Designed To Tell Us How Much Tax We Need To Pay

Reality: The tax code is written to incentivize economic stimulation and growth.

The Tax Code Is Designed To Tell Us How Much Tax We Need To Pay

Contrary to popular belief, the tax code is not simply designed for us to determine how much tax we owe. If that were the case we would simply pay a flat tax and it would be cut and dried. The tax code is actually there to provide us with tax benefits in exchange for spending time and money doing things that will be good for our economy. For most of us, this enables us to pay less tax by following the law. The wealthy understand that the tax code is full of those incentives, and most follow the law to the best of their ability, investing in ways that will help grow the economy. When we take advantage of incentives that are provided to us in the tax code, we are following the law, period. The laws are written for good reason, and the wealthy know that following those laws to the best of their ability is not only legal, but it's patriotic!

For those of us in the 2-15% of net worth in America, taxes are typically far and away the largest single expense for most people. Now, I don't mind paying taxes, but it is my opinion that our government is simply not a good steward of my money. Look around: the roads and airports are horribly antiquated, the trains and subways are filthy, people are living on the streets in most of our major cities, and our schools are ranked near the bottom in the developed world. When you think about it, we receive very little for what we put in. I was paying 50% of my income in taxes, and I was getting pretty angry about it. When I found out that people like Jared Kushner, Warren Buffet, and many, many of the 1% were paying little to no income tax, I wanted to know why and how they do it.

You see, we are conditioned to believe that somehow, if we follow the tax code and end up paying little or no income tax, that we are "gaming the system" and taking advantage of things. Like somehow we are doing something wrong or immoral.

Wouldn't everyone agree that it's a good thing for us to follow the laws of the land? If you believe that the laws of the United States of America are immoral, then we need to elect different lawmakers, and that's another issue altogether. However, it is patriotic to follow our laws, and the people who made them are supposedly much smarter than me. It is my civic duty to obey them. Investing in real estate is a fantastic way to honor our laws.

The government incentivizes us in various ways, and one of the most lucrative ways is using the tax code to your advantage with regards to real estate.

I have found that one of the easiest ways to do that is by investing in passive multifamily syndication. You see, when we have a business, the IRS allows us to defer our taxes via a technique called depreciation. When we buy anything FOR our business, we are able to take the estimated lifespan of that business tool and deduct a certain amount of that cost each year on our taxes. If a farmer purchases a tractor, then the cost of that tractor can offset his or her income from the farm for a certain number of years.

In addition, with our current tax law, the ENTIRE cost of some depreciable assets can be taken in year one, and if that cost doesn't offset all of the income from the farm, then the remaining amount can "carry forward" to offset future income. It's much like losses from the stock market, but when you sell the business you are required to "recapture" that depreciation, so you will pay taxes eventually.

With investment real estate, you have "things" that make up the asset, such as the roof, the parking lot, paint, furniture, etc. The costs of all of those things can be written off as depreciation in an investment property, and that figure can then be applied against the income of the asset.

I knew much of this from reading Rich Dad, Poor Dad, and our Brooklyn rental income, but finding houses or small multifamily buildings to invest in is a TON of work. You have to find the deal, get the loan, hire the lawyers, often do renovations, then either hire a management company or rent it out yourself. Once you screen tenants, then you have to deal with the tenants, and pay the taxes, expenses, and when they move out you start all over again. At the end of the day, you typically don't end up with cash flow either, or at least I wasn't able to make that work very well.

However, once I discovered the hidden opportunities in multifamily syndication, I learned that I could invest in large apartment complexes, make more income, and enjoy the tax benefits of depreciation. When I make a $100,000 investment in a multifamily syndication, the syndication sponsors do ALL of the work and I get the benefits of doing it myself, and I do nothing but collect the checks! The reason is simple, instead of buying a house you are getting together with other like-minded people and buying an entire apartment community. You own a part of it, you just don't have to run it day to day.

At the end of the year, instead of a 1099 where I have to pay taxes on the gains I've made, I receive what is called a K-1. That K-1 reflects all of the depreciation, which with our projects has often been anywhere from 30-60% of the original investment in year one. What I see often is thousands of dollars in gains in my pocket, but a tremendous loss on paper. What's left of that loss against that income may be used to defer gains on other rental real estates, and other passive income. What is not used may be carried over and used in subsequent years. I want to be clear that I still owe the taxes, I'm just deferring them. However, I can do that over and over, taking advantage of the incentives that our government gives us to invest in rental real estate.

So, over the past six years I've been investing passively in real estate along with the 1%, and by doing so I've saved more and more of my hard-earned tax dollars thanks to our real estate-friendly tax laws. By the time I retired from my career in market research, I was making six figures that was mostly tax-deferred from those investments, and my principle had doubled over the six years. Then, when we liquidate a project, the government allows something called a 1031 exchange. Most of the time we are able to purchase another apartment community, get more depreciation, and continue to offset taxes. We can do this again and again and again, making income, deferring taxes, while the property appreciates and our principle grows. When we exchange into a new property, that original $100,000 investment is often $110K - $150K or so, and the income goes up! When we die, the cost basis resets, (just like stocks, or a personal residence.), and our heirs start all over with a new tax basis. All of the deferred tax is forgiven. **THAT is how generational wealth is created, and THAT is one reason why and how the wealthy end up paying far fewer taxes than many of us.**

Today, I continue to invest and reinvest, with my passive income continuing to rise, paying much less tax than I used to. And my friends, that is how I retired and am able to write this book and help you do the same thing.

Why then, doesn't everyone do this? You guessed it, it's all about our mindset and how we are programmed to think about money. Our programming tells us that since this isn't widely known, we don't learn it at school, and we have to have a personal relationship with one or more of the general partners, that it must be a scam. We hear bad things in the news about people like Bernie Madoff running Ponzi schemes, but we never hear the stories of all of the successful private investments that transpire every day. Just remember, the news media likes to report the bad things, and the wealthiest people in America have been investing like this for decades. I didn't invent it; I'm only sharing what I've learned about it.

Here are some of the concerns that I have heard from my friends, colleagues, and family when I have presented opportunities that I plan to participate into them.

This is Too Good to be True

Think about when you invest in something like a public Real Estate Investment Trust, commonly known as a REIT. Many public REITs invest exactly like I have been doing, in syndications of multifamily apartment communities. The difference is that when you purchase shares in most publicly-traded REITs, you are buying shares in a fund that then invests in real estate, and along with it comes fees like most mutual funds. It takes a lot of money to pay the large wall street salaries, the millions of dollars that the manager makes whether you make money or not, the Manhattan offices, the millions of dollars in advertising…it goes on and on. With private syndication, the sponsor typically collects 3% of the purchase price as an acquisition fee, as opposed to an average of 9%.[1]

Most of the private syndications that I invest in, don't make much above the initial acquisition fee until the limited partner investors make their promised, or preferred, returns. Even more, the acquisition fee is usually shared amongst several general partners, and it compensates them for finding the deal, underwriting the deal, working with investors, doing due diligence, and everything else that needs to get done to acquire the asset. The proceeds above the preferred return are shared via a split that favors the investors, usually 70/30 or so to start. When you eliminate all of the expenses of wall street there is a lot left over to share. That is why private investments very often have returns that are far above public investments. It's only a myth that they are "too good to be true,"

This must be illegal and/or immoral

I've covered this above, but you should speak with your CPA about your particular situation. I am only sharing my experience, but I can tell you that I haven't seen a CPA yet that doesn't say that multifamily syndications can't be a great thing if done properly. I've never met a financial advisor that didn't tell his clients

NOT to do one. Why? First, he or she doesn't want to lose the business, but most likely they've never heard of this hidden investment either. I don't invest in anything that I haven't researched and made sure that everything has been structured within SEC guidelines.

This is Too Risky

The big "aha" moment for me was when I realized that, although I could theoretically tell you how the stock market works, at the end of the day, whether I invested in what I believed was a strong stock was an educated roll of the dice. There was no way that I could understand the risk factors of a particular industry, let alone an individual stock or an even more complicated mutual fund. Even when I have actually worked at a public company, and that company was healthy and profitable, the stock purchase plan that I invested in went down! I worked there, thought that I knew the business, and I still didn't pick it right! With real estate, I've gained a much better understanding of the risks so that I can mitigate them myself, or make sure that the general partners in a passive investment are mitigating them for me. We buy in markets where we can cash flow, raise enough capital for reserves, secure a loan that we don't have to get out of at the wrong time and go in with 30% or more equity on day one. I'll talk more about risk later in this book, but my highest-risk investments today are definitely stocks.

I like investments where I have control

This is a good one. We all know people who have purchased real estate with the intention of building something, but who quickly run into trouble. The town doesn't want to issue the permit, or the zoning board won't approve the rezoning, or the economy crashes and they can't afford to build.

The property sits there, but there are still taxes to be paid. What about that house that you are going to fix up, and you open up the floor and find a giant sinkhole under it and you have to fill it in and completely rebuild the foundation? I saw that on a TV show about house flipping. What if the city decides to close the amazing school that is right down the road, and your new zoned school is not only far away, it's ranked one of the worst schools in the state? That happened to me with our home in upstate New York. Almost any investment has elements that can't be controlled.

One thing about real estate though, it's not liquid. That said, if someone truly wants out we do our best to find another investor to take their place. With any other real estate that you may think you "control," it's probably not very liquid either. You have to put it on the market, hire a realtor, and go through all of the hassle I mentioned above. There is no such thing as true control.

Now when I hear about some of the wealthiest people in our country paying very little tax, I understand that they are following our laws and that you and I can do the same thing if we are willing to open our minds and learn about hidden investments. At the end of the day, when we buy an apartment community we are adding value to the economy. We create income, we pay taxes, we hire contractors and management companies, and all kinds of jobs are created and living conditions improved. I feel good about that, and the government does too. What real estate adds to our economy is more than my taxes used to cover, so everyone can have a better life. (And remember, I'm only deferring those taxes, it's just that I can continue to do that via tax laws that have been there for years and years.)

Today, the investments that I rely on for income, wealth preservation, and tax savings are in real estate syndications with very conservative amounts of leverage. My longer-term "risky" money is in stocks. I plan to continue doing what I'm doing, living off the income that is produced, and educating and sharing the opportunities that I plan to invest in. Deferring taxes as much as possible all the way.

CHAPTER 4:
Myth #4
Manage Your Wealth And Leave A Legacy By Diversifying Your Investments

> **Reality: Standard Financial Planning doesn't care about legacies – the process is designed for us to die broke.**

I call it Retirement Roulette. Go online and pull up almost any financial Calculator. About 90 percent of them will ask you how long you expect to be retired.

Financial advisors typically ask a similar question when they put retirement plans together for you. What they are really asking us is, "Tell us when you think you will die, and we will make an educated guess about how long you MAY have before the money runs out."

The retirement road map that we are given by the financial services industry, in our workplaces, and at home in our formative years is designed for us to die with nothing left. When my parents were planning for their retirement, they used 90 years as their number. They both died aged 81, and between that and the economy—oops—they didn't even come close.

There is a commercial running right now from a major financial services firm that starts with: "Tell us how much you have and how long you need it to last, and we will tell you how much you can spend." In real-time you can watch your balance go down and see how many years you can keep going. I don't know about you, but that is not how I want to spend my retirement.

If this standard way that we are supposed to plan for retirement is so great, then why are there so many businesses that are thriving helping people fill the gap between what they have saved and what they need? Let's dive into the numbers.

We're going to use a retirement calculator provided by bankrate.com, but almost any financial calculator will work similarly.

(https://www.bankrate.com/calculators/retirement/retirement-plan-calculator.aspx)

Since this particular retirement calculator isn't special in any way, and I urge you to try out a couple of different options to get a sense of what I'm showing you. The service Bankrate offers is almost identical to the hundreds of retirement calculator versions out there, but they do a very good job of search optimization. They were at or near the top of the search results! I simply searched for "Retirement financial calculator," I'll use this one to demonstrate what I'm talking about.

I've put a scenario together for a single person that needs an annual income of $150K in retirement and has $1M in their 401K when they retire at 65. According to the results, if they achieve a 10 percent return, and that's a BIG IF, they'd better not live past the age of 78. That means, to maintain anything close to their current lifestyle they have 13 years left before going broke.

Now let's say the market only returns 5 percent. A five percent return is far more realistic, once taxes and fees are deducted. Now that person only gets to live until they are 74. Nine more years.

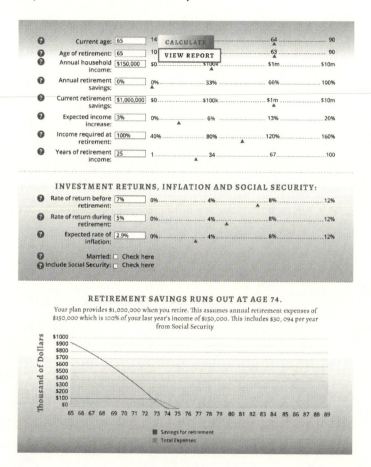

You can play around with your particular situation and goals, using this or any other calculator, but you get the general idea. We really don't know what is going to happen with the market, and realistically, there is very little that we can do to mitigate risk except settle for 1-3 percent returns in CDs or money market funds.

And with our money in those vehicles, the outlook becomes particularly grim.

Most common retirement calculators rely on complicated algorithms based upon returns, regular withdrawals, social security, and many other variables that depend upon the stock market. On top of that, there are dozens of factors outside of our control, such as whether social security will remain steady, what will happen to tax rates, and the state of the economy.

We all know from statistics 101, the more variables there are, the harder things are to predict. The key to mitigating risk is to control as many variables as we can, and although we are conditioned to believe that some investments are "safe," the reality is that publicly traded investments offer very little in the way of true risk mitigation.

By the way, another myth that the professionals will tell you is that when we retire our expenses go down. I don't know about you, but after 35 years of having 2 weeks of vacation and often working even during that, I don't want to spend my retirement in a downsized house and never go anywhere. In retirement, at the very least I want to keep the income that I have today, and for most of us those expenses will only go up as the years go by.

Real Estate Offers Control

With real estate, it is possible to mitigate risk to a far greater extent. There are steps and measures built into the process to help reduce risk. Investors can reduce the amount of leverage, secure longer-term loans that won't come due at the wrong time and make sure that the property begins cash flowing from day one. We will dive deeper into risk mitigation later in the book, but this idea is radical for many people who have lived by conventional wisdom their entire lives.

What if, instead of investing 100 percent of your retirement funds into the public stock market, instead you invested in private, cash-flowing investments?

That's exactly what I began to do six years ago. I moved roughly $700K of my savings from the stock market and invested it into seven multifamily syndications over a three year period. Those seven investments generated around $50K in passive, tax-deferred income annually, which I used to invest in more syndications that generated more passive income. In year two we refinanced two properties, which resulted in around $80,000 returned to me, in addition to my other income. I turned right around and invested that into another syndication. We liquidated two properties in the third year, and my capital was returned plus another 20 percent.

I took those profits and rolled them into what is known as a 1031 exchange, which is a new property where I could reinvest the money and continue to defer taxes. For those two properties, my $100K investment in each had turned into $250K, (plus the income I had made over the hold period), and the new investments now paid me a higher income. In just three years, my principle had grown to over $1.3M, and my income was just shy of $100K, still tax-deferred. Shocked? So was I!

Over the next three years I continued this process of investing and deferring, and today my principal is well over 1.5M, my income is well into the six figures, I continue to defer taxes, and the principle can be left to my family when I die.

When that happens, the cost basis will be reset, and based on our tax laws today they will start over with a clean slate relative to taxes, and inherit a six-figure income. Along the way, we've created countless numbers of good jobs, given hundreds and hundreds of hard-working Americans better places to live, and we've helped investors change their lives as mine has changed.

Contrast that with the strategy that my parents employed. They had $700,000 when they retired, and they put it into stocks that were supposedly safe but would continue to grow. That money, along with other investments put them around $1M in the late 1980s. I can remember when my father retired. His company gave him a choice between taking a lump sum payment or receiving a pension. Everyone told him to take the lump sum, the stock market returns more, and his financial advisor was simply giddy over the prospect of handling his money. I remember when he chose the lump sum, my mother told me: "This is so much better because we will be able to leave you and your brother a big part of it." They wanted nothing more, and we've been programmed to believe that mutual funds, annuities, and bonds will enable us to do that. That's what we hear, but what they are really telling us is to save, and live on that savings until we die or run out of money. In our heads we believe, as my parents did, that at a 10% average return in the market that they were going to make $80,000 annually to live on, and leave their children a good chunk of the million dollars. Looking back at the market returns during those years, how much they had, and how much they needed to live, it was really always going to last around 15-20 years. The market is volatile, and especially when it's down you must sell the stocks to secure the income you need. Once that happens it's gone, and you have less…a vicious cycle. Their advisors didn't tell them that though. They told them that it would pay them an average of 10% while continuing to grow. Technically that is true, but it's not the whole story. For things to happen like that you need a lot of timing and luck.

Fortunately, both my brother and I are doing fine and we were able to help them as the end grew closer.

After they died, I was going through their things and found a folder I hadn't seen before. My father, in the last year of his life, was calculating how long the money would last before he would have to sell the house. It was heartbreaking, and I vowed right then and there that I was going to do everything I could to keep my daughter from that situation. You can do the same by changing your beliefs and mindset.

Most of the ultra-wealthy have a world view that dramatically impacts their succession plan, and they plan to NOT die broke. In addition to a comfortable retirement, they want to leave their heirs something at the end. The wealthy know how to do this, and that is how their wealth is preserved for generations to come.

They know that building and maintaining generational wealth requires investing into income-producing assets, and using and thinking about money strategically. I've found these tactics that a majority of the 1% employ to be especially helpful on my road to financial freedom.

Most of the Wealthiest People Have Multiple Income Streams

One of the biggest eye-openers for me was the idea of multiple income streams. Most of the one percent know better than to rely on one single source for their income. I know now to do that, and I receive my income from passive real estate investments, active real estate investments, I have a few consulting clients, and my husband has a pension from the police department. My goal is to diversify into even more income streams in the years to come via other hidden investments in addition to multifamily syndications.

Most of the 1 percent live below their means

Have you ever noticed what Mark Zuckerberg, Bill Gates, or Warren Buffet wear most of the time? I never, if ever, see them flash their wealth around. Most of the time, the very wealthy buy things that will appreciate or at least hold their value. They invest in appreciating assets and make sure that they are living below their means. They are savers, and always have significant prudent reserves on hand in case things that they can't control go bad.

The top 1 percent pay themselves first

No matter what the revenue stream, the first thing that should happen is that you should take something off the top and invest it in cash-flowing assets, or even smart stocks if it makes sense. Once you have a solid amount set aside for reserve funds, put that money to work! Your money should be working for you, growing. If your money is stagnant, it is losing value through inflation.

The 1% are financially literate and are always further educating themselves

Most of the wealthy are lifetime learners. They are continuously seeking new information and resources that will help them keep a leg up on the competition. The world of finance isn't static, and the best practices today may not be the smartest tactics of tomorrow. By always learning, you ensure that you remain alert and ready to change as economic conditions change. And your friends will very often come to you seeking advice on the newest investment opportunities!

The 1% are willing to take calculated risks

They do their research to minimize those risks, but part of being so successful is embracing the unknown. If you know the risks you can begin to mitigate them. The wealthy keep an open mind and aren't afraid to take calculated risks.

The 1% embrace partnerships

Allies are a sure-fire way to grow your wealth. They help mitigate risk, grow the scope of an investment, and offer insight into deals and opportunities that might otherwise pass you by. Always be looking to make new friends and business partners.

The flip side of that is to be careful who you work with. Choose carefully, and always verify. As you know, when I began investing in real estate syndications it was through a colleague that I trusted. My objective was simply not to lose money and help him. What followed was so much more than that, and I was eventually able to partner with him and launch my career as an investor!

The 1% know their worth and the worth of others

Some advice is worth paying top dollar for. When it comes down to ensuring success in an investment, cheaper advice is not often the best route. What I pay my accountant, what I pay my coach, what I pay to belong to mastermind groups to make contacts and meet experts that I can emulate, are some of the best investments I have made. The wealthy know this, and most of all they know the value of their own time. I spend less and less time with activities that can be delegated. Too often do I see my friends doing things that they could easily have someone else do while they spend their time on activities that are most valuable.

For me to do this required a shift in my mindset. I always thought that paying someone to do something that I could easily do myself was a waste of money. I know now that the truly wealthy know how to outsource tasks that are not high value, and they spend their time on things that will help them grow or that they particularly enjoy.

I still spend time on activities that aren't high value, but I spend much less on those things than I used to. I now know that the process of reprogramming my mind is an essential step towards growing my net worth. Today, time is my most valuable asset. I can't get more of it.

CHAPTER 5:

Myth #5

Your 401K Will Grow Tax-Free And Provide You With A Wonderful Retirement

> **Reality: That 401K is probably not going to get you through your golden years.**

When I began my career in the late 1980s, pension plans were just beginning to be phased out in favor of the 401K. The working class fell for it, hook line and sinker because on the surface it sounded fantastic. We could save for retirement right out of our paycheck, and not even notice the deductions. Many companies would match what we contributed, and then whatever we put away would lower our taxable income, creating immediate tax savings. Then, our earnings would grow tax-free, and by the end of our career our 401k, combined with social security, would provide us with a long, glorious retirement.

We were told to start early and to put the maximum into the plan. For the first 5-10 years of my career, like most of us were, I was in a low tax bracket, so my taxes were of course lower overall. Even so, by putting the most in my 401K and enjoying the employer match at 3-5% or so, I was sure that I was well on my way. The 401K, and the fact that I put the most I possibly could in it, was not a bad thing, it's just that it's not the fantastic deal that we were sold. Employers pay less today and take on far less risk than they used to when they offered traditional pension plans, and we are now responsible for picking up the slack.

You see, an important fact simply didn't register with me until I began to help my parents with their finances. Years and years later, when we go to collect our money, that money isn't taxed as capital gains. Growing "tax-free" doesn't mean that you don't pay taxes, it simply means that you don't have to pay capital gains as the fund managers buy and sell stocks within the fund. (More on that later.) Taxes rarely decrease, and when we retire, most of us will be taxed in a MUCH higher tax bracket than when we were at the beginning of our careers. We are often told that we will need less money when we retire, and for most of us, that is patently false, unless we are willing to dramatically downsize our lifestyle. Most of us do indeed want to keep our standard of living when we finally need that money, those withdrawals are taxed as full earned income in our current tax bracket, at whatever the tax rates are at the time. If we had simply put the money in stocks, it would at least be taxed at the capital gains rate, but 401K distributions are taxed as regular income at whatever the tax rates are when we take it out. If you know and internalize this, your relationship with your 401k will be altered forever. In short, we put the money in when our tax liability is low, and take it out when we are in a higher tax bracket. The government takes as much as they possibly can from your retirement plan.

I want to travel, play golf (but first get better), spend time with my family, and do my best to stay active and healthy, because if I'm lucky there will come a time when I will need help. If I'm fortunate to live to a ripe old age, when the time comes when my husband and/or

I can't live alone without that help, that's when I'd better plan for the bills to really start to roll in. To keep my parents at home, just the help was costing $25-$50K annually, and that was before buying food and other necessities.

To add insult to injury, even if we don't need the 401K money right away, the government forces us to withdraw it regardless. They want their tax revenue, so they make you withdraw a certain amount based upon your age and life expectancy.

Some of us are lucky, and our jobs offer a company match. If your company offers that, you should absolutely take advantage of it. Just understand that with most companies, that 401K match vests based upon how long you stay with the company, with a certain percentage vesting each year. Of course, the company can lay you off at any time, and in most states, they can get rid of you for almost any reason. Anything that is not "vested" you lose, so in most cases that money isn't real until you can take it with you. Now, many companies in America are fantastic, and there are certainly exceptions to the above. The point is, nothing is guaranteed, and the more that you rely on your company to make sure that you have a wonderful retirement, the better the chance is that it might not end up the way you expect it to. All plans are not alike either.

Since all plans are not the same, before going all-in on your company's 401 plan, do some digging. There are numerous resources that can help you learn the potential drawbacks, but here are a few immediate questions to ask. If you don't know the answer to some or most of these, it may be time to reevaluate your retirement plan.

Question 1: How complete is your investment lineup?

In a 401k, a well-rounded investment lineup should include most if not all of the following:

Money-market or stable-value funds, which are conservative options that focus on protection. Large-cap equity fund: This is a large fund that invests in big, stable companies.

Mid-cap equity fund: These invest in middle-sized companies with potential for growth, and thus a bigger upside.

Small-cap equity fund: This revolves around small companies with high potential for rapid growth. These are often riskier.

Fixed-income fund: This is made up of intermediate-term corporate and government bonds A diverse portfolio will mix various types of equity and income funds because they each tend to react differently depending on the market cycle.

You also need to ask about fees, management options, accessibility, so you should always weigh your potential options before committing fully to the first plan your company offers. If your company has a match though, many suggest that you fund the plan up to the match and then invest the rest in other investments. Additionally, a majority of you are already in the top tax bracket in a high-tax state like I am. In that case it may make more sense to take the maximum deduction now, but only you can decide what is best for your particular situation. A good tax advisor is so important, so make sure that you get the best advice possible.

Now, in 2001, the government did realize that we were saving tax when we needed it least and paying more tax when we needed most, and their solution was something called a Roth 401k. Roth 401ks are funded with after-tax dollars, but they are not taxed at all when you withdraw the money in retirement. They are amazing, but there are income limits to participate, and if you are reading this there is a very good chance that you make too much money to participate in a Roth. I wasn't eligible, and most accredited investors are not able to take advantage of it either.

However, if you have a Roth account, when you retire, your withdrawals won't be taxed at all, and this is a huge advantage. This means that anything that you make in a Roth account grows tax-free, but is also tax-free when you take it out. However, you do pay taxes now, before you put the money in. With a Roth, the idea is to pay the tax now, but not to pay it when you take it out. It can be a game-changer if you qualify to do it.

Whether or not your 401K is a Roth or a standard investment account, it's still almost impossible to escape the fees. What's scary about that is that most people don't believe that 401(k) plans actually charge fees at all! A recent study from TD Ameritrade[2] found that 37% of people don't believe they pay any 401(k) fees, 22% didn't know about fees and 14% don't understand how to determine what fees they pay!

Fees, fees, and more fees

Hidden fees can sink your retirement before it even starts. The fees that come with every step of standard retirement planning eat away at your nest egg every year, and some can cut your 401(k) earnings by 30-50 percent throughout a career.

A 2019 investigation showed that A 401(k) typically has more than a dozen fees that are undisclosed and that these can greatly impact an account's returns. These fees, many of which as we know are found in almost all mutual funds, are trustee fees, bookkeeping fees, finder's fees, and legal fees, and mostly arise from two sources: the corporate plan provider, and the individual funds specific to each plan. All of these occur in addition to any prospect or trading fees. We will dive into mutual fund fees in more detail in chapter six, but I want you to begin to understand those that are specific to your 401K and the potency of even a 1 or 2 percent loss over 20-plus years.

Mutual funds within a 401(k) will often take a 2 percent fee right off the top. That means, if your fund is up 7 percent for the year but charges a 2 percent fee, you're left with 5 percent. The 2 percent fee taken off the top can end up costing hundreds of thousands of dollars by the time you retire.

Fees of only 1% per year can slash the value of your savings by 28 percent over the next 35 years, according to a Department of Labor report. [3]

Looking at the past five years, The Motley Fool, a well-respected financial advisement company, saw an average 401(k) return of just over 7%. While that may sound at first like a good return, compare that to a near 15% return[4] over the same timeframe for the S&P – meaning the average 401(k) returned less than half of the return of a broad-based index.

Most of the experts tell us that a return of 5-8 percent per year in your 401K is a good number to use for planning. 5-8 percent? What happened to the 10 percent average that the market usually returns over time? The short answer is that it's been swallowed by fees. Even those who are optimizing their 401K contributions with careful tax breaks and employer matches will find that 10 percent, especially after taxes, is just not realistic. With a Roth you will at least save the taxes, but the fees will almost certainly be there.

Rollover and Self-Directed IRAs

For those of us who change jobs every four or five years, we can roll over our 401K into what's known as a "Rollover IRA." All it means is that we move it out of the company 401K plan and into a custodian of our choosing, whether that is a brokerage or even a traditional bank. Once you get the money out of your old company and into an IRA that you control, there is a hidden option that most people have never heard of called a "Checkbook IRA," sometimes referred to as an SDIRA or Self-Directed IRA. Very few people know about SDIRAs, and they offer a lot of value to people who have a rollover IRA and want to invest in hidden investments beyond wall street.

With a Checkbook or SDIRA, you are free to invest your retirement money the way that YOU want to, but you have to be very disciplined and very careful because if you make a mistake and not follow the IRS guidelines it could cost you big time.

Those guidelines include terms such as you can invest in real estate, but it must be passive, you can't use it yourself or any work on it yourself, you can't partner with most of your relatives and countless other stipulations. The IRS is serious, and if you violate the rules you could have to pay taxes and penalties on your entire IRA. However, if you are responsible enough to manage your own money and follow the guidelines, an entire investing world is open to you.

With an SDIRA you can buy gold, real estate, mortgages, do private lending, or simply open up a brokerage account if that's what you'd like to do. I've used mine to purchase mortgages, lend private money to experienced people who do house fix and flips, invest in startup companies, and I've invested in two private funds. And of course, I've invested in multifamily syndications as well. All I can tell you is that once I took control of my retirement funds, they've been growing a lot faster than when my investment options limited to what the financial services firm that held my IRA allowed me to access.

Many people are misguided by investment companies that are more concerned with keeping as many customers as possible. When you ask them they may tell you that you already have a self-directed account, but that is only partly true. Most brokerages will tell you that your account is "self-directed", but what they mean is that you are free to invest in products that THEY OFFER. You are still limited within their offerings. Many companies will help you set up one of these special IRAs, and you should be able to search online to find them, along with articles about the pros and cons of them. A true SDIRA has many rules to follow, but if you follow those rules to the letter, you can invest in opportunities that are hidden to most of us.

I moved a portion of my retirement funds into an SDIRA many years ago, and it is one of the best moves I ever made.

No matter how much is in your IRA, self-directed or not, you will pay fees, and unless it's a Roth you will pay taxes on top of that. Don't let that be a surprise like my parents did. Plan for it, and work with tax professionals to decide what is best for your particular situation.

Here Comes the Annuity

Now that you've begun to see some of the downsides of standard 401K plans and IRAs, your advisors and the media will most likely convince you to turn your attention to the dreaded annuity. You will hear many sources tell you that annuities are the best way to "guarantee" steady income for your retirement. Yes, it's usually guaranteed, but make no mistake, that guarantee comes with a hefty price tag.

Almost without exception, financial advisors make higher commissions from selling annuities than almost any other financial product, and, consequently, 401Ks fees look like a downright bargain compared to the typical annuity. That said, there are many types of annuities, just as there are many types of mutual funds. They are all quite different, and some are more expensive than others.

Annuities are a vehicle that you purchase, usually from an insurance company, and then the company goes out and invests that money, paying a guaranteed fixed amount back to you. Some annuities actually keep the money when you die, some have a death benefit, but all of them take your money and invest in many of the hidden investments that are not offered to the masses, and then pay you a minimum amount. They keep the rest. They often find investments that yield them 15% or more, (like many hidden investments regularly do), and they pay you the 4%-7% that you agreed to and they keep the difference. I prefer to go straight to the hidden, cash-flowing investments, but most insurance companies won't tell you that of course. The good news is that you are guaranteed to make that minimum, so it's safe in that sense. (By the way, this is usually what the banks do as well. You put your money in, they turn around and invest it in places that are hidden from most of us.)

You give an insurance company your savings and they, in return, pay you a steady income. In many annuities, if you die before you've received all of your payments, the insurance company keeps the money. Additionally, there are typically stiff fees if you need early access to the money. There are all kinds of ways that the insurance industry can put these annuities together, so make sure that you read the fine print and understand what you are getting into.

Smart people every day invest in annuities because they hear how safe they are, and believe that they are a way to enjoy safe and risk-free income. And guess what? I have one too. I set it up years ago before learning any of this. It's what I was wired to do!

I have a very good friend who is an educated, accomplished professional, with a very important job with lots of responsibility, who bought a $500,000 annuity that will pay her a fixed 7% for the rest of her life. This may sound ideal, but it comes with some serious drawbacks.

First and foremost, that is 7% that is taxed as ordinary income, which means that it's probably more like 4-5% at the end of the day. Either way, she'll get $35,000 annually that is taxed, and the company has her $500,000 to invest. She also isn't entirely sure what type of annuity it actually is. She just knows that she will have to pay a huge penalty to get out of it.

With her other funds, she invested a smaller sum in a multifamily syndication that pays an 8% preferred return. A $500,000 investment into that particular syndication would yield $40,000+ annually that is tax-deferred, while her principle remained intact and will more than likely appreciate considerably. Compare those two investment options and you tell me which sounds safer and a better long-term option.

Now, not ALL syndications make money right away, the returns are not at all guaranteed, and not all annuities are the same. Annuities are one of the few investments that can yield guaranteed income, but it's an expensive guarantee, and only you know if that peace of mind is worth it for your particular situation.

It is very important for all of us to take the time to get smart about our retirement income options. Trust me -- it's the difference between a wonderful retirement or a miserable one. Don't just take my word for it, spend some time to research and determine what is best for YOU.

CHAPTER 6:
Myth #6
Put Your Money In No Load Funds And Avoid High Fees

Reality: Those No-Load Funds are loaded with fees galore.

Most of the information in this chapter holds true for mutual funds that are in your 401K. Add the 401k fees that we talked about in the last chapter on top of the fees that we are going to talk about in this one! Most mutual funds have plenty of fees of their own whether they are inside or outside of your 401K or IRA.

Remember, the wealthy think about money logically, so let's take a step back and think about the financial services industry in general. There are hundreds of no-load mutual funds offered by every firm imaginable, most of whom have the best intentions. However, above all else, the majority are public companies, with shareholders of their own. They exist not to make you rich, but to turn a profit themselves. Some are more expensive than others, and many promote their low fees—some advertise that they have no fees at all. But even they have to make money somewhere, right?

Brokerage firms spend hundreds of millions of dollars every year in advertising, and the money to pay for all of that advertising has to come from somewhere. Most firms have brick and mortar locations all over the country, TD Ameritrade alone, at the time of writing this, has over 300 retail branches in the US. Yet they, along with many others like them, advertise that they are "commission-free." Realistically, there have to be fees somewhere along the line, but you often have to dig deep to find them. (By the way, I trade stocks through my TD Ameritrade account. They are a good company, but you should absolutely know everything that you are getting into. Even though they say no fees, they are making money via the spread and I'm sure lots of other places. The point is to be aware of that and invest accordingly.)

Take a no-load fund for example. A no-load fund simply means that the fund itself does not charge a separate fee within the fund get into it or get out of it. However, all funds have fees, even no-load funds, and it is often simply a question of how and when we the investors pay for them. There is a wide range of hidden costs, but ultimately all of them cost us money. Sometimes those costs can eat away at over half of your actual returns.

The three most common fees are commissions, management fees, and operating fees.

Commissions represent the transaction costs of buying and selling shares, and often a large portion of that commission will go to the broker or salesperson. They may be calculated in different ways, depending upon the investment product.

Management fees, also known as investment advisory fees or account maintenance fees, are the ongoing charges for managing the assets of the investment fund. They are generally stated as a percentage of the cost of the assets invested in the fund. Sometimes management fees are also used to cover administrative expenses. The cost of management fees will vary, depending on the company and the investment product itself.

Operating fees cover all other services, such as recordkeeping, upkeep, and investment advice. This is anything involved in the day-to-day management of investment products. They also may be stated either as a flat fee or as a percentage of the investment. All of these fees drain your savings each and every year.

Most funds, even if they charge no upfront or back-end commissions, are what are called "actively managed" funds. This means that a fund manager works daily, buying, and selling stocks within the funds to maximize the returns. The problem is, very seldom does all of that buying and selling translate to more money for investors.

In 2008, billionaire Warren Buffet famously challenged a large and powerful hedge fund to a 1-million-dollar bet. Buffett's contention ultimately proved successful and showed that including all fees and hidden costs, a standard S&P 500 index fund would outperform a hand-picked portfolio of funds over a 10-year period.

Tony Robbins writes about actively managed "no load" funds in his book, Unshakeable. According to Robbins, if an actively managed mutual fund is held outside of a 401K or IRA, the average costs are actually over 3% a year. Add in taxes, and that 3% easily becomes 4% or more.

ADD 'EM UP

Nontaxable Account
Expense ratio: 0.90%
Transaction costs: 1.44%
Cash drag: 0.83%

Total costs: 3.17%

Taxable Account
Expense ratio: 0.90%
Transaction costs: 1.44%
Cash drag: 0.83%
Tax cost: 1.00%

Total costs: 4.17%

"The Real Cost of Owning a Mutual Fund," Forbes, April 4, 2011

* This table was taken from the book *Unshakable* by Tony Robbins

Even if the fund advertises an expense ratio that says it is less than 3%, many fees are simply not included in that number. (The expense ratio is calculated by dividing a fund's operating expenses by the average dollar value of its assets under management, meaning the portfolios themselves.) Those costs are hidden and accumulate on top of the expense ratio fees.

Passively managed funds, sometimes called index funds or ITFs, typically carry lower expense ratios and have fewer fees overall because those funds are designed to simply mirror exchange indices as opposed to trading stocks in and out trying to pick the winners and losers. Because of that, actively managed funds can rack up two or three times as many fees. However, whether active or passive, all mutual funds charge management fees to cover their operating costs, such as the cost of hiring and retaining managers who oversee the funds. Together, the operating fees and management fees make up the expense ratios. There are gross expense ratios and net expense ratios, and all kinds of other fees. You really must read the fine print, and not surprisingly, most companies make it extremely difficult to find and track down all of that fine print.

To put it simply, the cost of operating the company is funded by **your** savings. Meanwhile, hard data **has proved many times,** that professional investors/fund managers are rarely more effective than a standard S&P 500 index fund.

The database from Credit Suisse Hedge Fund Index on hedge fund performance is extremely illuminating, and it still stands today as one of the most comprehensive looks at the industry. In a 24-year span -- from January 1994 to October 2018 -- the S&P 500 Index outperformed **every major hedge fund strategy** by about 2.25 percent in annualized return, according to Investopedia.[5] That occurred through some of the highest highs and lowest lows in economic history, and it demonstrated what countless other studies have repeatedly shown: actively managed funds rely on fortuitous timing and a few true, genius managers to ever be more profitable than the market.

Even Vanguard, who pioneered the low-cost index fund, and has no physical retail locations, can cost investors serious money. The company fees that you may not notice for some funds such as a $50 short-term redemption fee, a $20 fee for transactions by mutual funds that aren't on the broker's NTF list, a recurring $30 annual fee for cash management accounts below one million dollars, and numerous other charges that can stack up over a decade or more of investing. And Vanguard is one of the most affordable index funds out there, offering some of the lowest expense ratios on the market, and they still have numerous additional fees.

Even with the "lowest-cost" funds, you typically don't get a bill explaining how much of your savings went toward paying fund expenses, because most of those costs are paid directly out of each fund's returns. Vanguard, and companies like them, definitely cost less, but no doubt we are paying something, even when there are apparently "no fees." They have to make money somehow.

Imagine my surprise when this all came together and I realized the following:

A. I was paying far more in hidden fees than I thought.

B. I was paying taxes every time the fund manager, who may or may not have been adding value, bought and sold stocks within the funds. (Hence my $65,000 tax bill.)

The wealthy know all of this. The wealthy also have access to products and funds that the rest of us don't even know about. Most brokerages have a separate division for "ultra-high net worth" individuals." For the most part, those are investors whose net worth is more than $30M. Vanguard says it explicitly on their website. "As your assets with us increase—from $5 million to $50 million and beyond —your team will expand too, providing you with the additional support you need."

Wealth fund managers in the U.S. are rapidly adding additional staff and services to focus attention on serving the top 1 percent, according to a 2019 article from PENTA. By offering specialized services, they are trying to draw in these high-end clients.

Why? Because these clients represent a much higher profit margin. One bank said wealth management for ultra-high-net-worth clients typically generates returns on investment of more than 30%, compared to returns of greater than 15% for high-net-worth clients and returns in the range of 10% to 15% for the merely wealthy.

How do those with $30M+ net worth individuals regularly receive returns of 20-30% while the rest of us are happy with half of that? Relatively lower fees a small role, but overwhelmingly it comes down to access to investments that the rest of us simply don't know about. These **hidden investments,** one of them being private multifamily syndications, are what allow for such lucrative returns.

When I first heard about the returns that some multifamily syndications and other hidden investments were achieving regularly, I was convinced that I was not being told the truth. The fact is, for the wealthiest Americans, returns in the ballpark of 30 percent are a regular occurrence. We don't believe that it is possible to get the kind of returns that Ultra High Net Worth individuals and family offices receive, because the investments that they participate in are hidden from us. To even find out that these UHNW management departments even exist requires searching far beyond the first page or two of Google results. Then, before you can find out the details you must show that you are eligible for the club.

Yes, to even speak with anyone, you must first qualify to get in.

Given all of that, what should we as the top 2-15% make of all this? First, now that we know to read the fine print, we must search it out and read it. Second, we should gather information from other sources in addition to what our brokerage firms tell us.

In *Unshakeable*, Tony Robbins lists the core four principles that should guide every single investment decision that we make:

1. Don't lose money

2. Make sure that the potential rewards VASTLY outweigh the risks

3. Make sure that the investment is tax-efficient – the only thing that matters is what you get to keep at the end. (Remember my $65,000 in capital gains when I didn't take out any money?)

4. Diversify

The top 1 percent know that you can have a conservative investment and still have great returns. Personally, since my expertise is in real estate, I look for real estate investments that are already cash-flowing, are not heavily leveraged, have opportunities for depreciation and expense deductions to reduce taxes, and I diversify between markets, operators, and other real estate investments like self-storage, commercial spaces, and mortgage notes. In addition to real estate, I also invest in cash-flowing private businesses, precious metals, and oil and gas. (Look for my next book to learn about some of those things in detail!)

I'm still in the stock market, and remember that annuity? The last time I looked it was going to cost me way too much to get out of it. Fortunately, I don't have a lot invested in mine, and I'm approaching the age where I can investigate the options I have to withdraw from it without penalties. I'll keep everyone posted on how that goes.

CHAPTER 7:

Myth #7

Trust The Experts

Reality: "The Air is Safe at Ground Zero" – The Experts Don't Necessarily Know

On the morning of September 11, 2001, I landed at 6am at Newark airport on a redeye flight from San Diego, where I had been on a business trip. I was glad to be home. It was going to be a beautiful day in New York, and as the cab took me towards the Holland Tunnel, I saw the sun coming up over Lower Manhattan on my way to my apartment in Greenwich Village. There was an election that day, and I planned to take a nap, and then head over to vote on my way to my office that afternoon. I had just dozed off when my husband called me and told me to turn on the TV. He said that a plane had just hit the World Trade Center. The rest of the day, and the day after that, and the weeks and even months that followed were simply surreal. I've never been so afraid and so lost. For me, nothing before or after that experience comes even close to the terror, helplessness, and sheer horror as I saw people jumping from the buildings that day, and for days after, seeing the fighter jets patrolling the skies above the city.

As Americans do, the entire country pulled together in the face of crisis. Everyone wanted to help. First Responders from all over the country came to assist at the site of the collapsed World Trade Center, methodically combing through the still-smoldering rubble. Each night, the Fire Department would spray down the streets of Lower Manhattan in an effort to keep the soot and debris down as much as possible. Three months later, when my family came from Texas for Christmas, the site, now famously known around the world as Ground Zero, was still smoldering.

Scientists from all over the country came to New York to test the air quality. Three short days after the collapse, Christine Todd Whitman, the head of the Environmental Protection Agency, told reporters, "The good news continues to be that air samples we have taken have all been at levels that cause us no concern." On Sept. 18, 2001, she reassured residents that their air "is safe to breathe and their water is safe to drink."

Since then, my husband has retired from his position in the New York City Police Department, and we have attended countless funerals of police officers, firemen, and friends and family who have developed cancers and debilitating lung diseases.

On the 15th anniversary of the attacks, Whitman apologized to those affected saying, "Whatever we got wrong, we should acknowledge, and people should be helped," she said, adding that she still "feels awful" about the tragedy and its aftermath. "I'm very sorry that people are sick," she said. "I'm very sorry that people are dying and if the EPA and I in any way contributed to that, I'm sorry. We did the very best we could at the time with the knowledge we had." It was later revealed that the EPA had conflicting internal data on the air quality that was not released to the public back in 2001 and was effectively ignored—compromising the health of countless individuals.

The impact of this faulty information from the experts continues to be felt by tens of thousands of rescue workers almost two decades later.

At the end of the day, humans can only do the best with the information that we have. I share this story to highlight an important idea: the experts do not always provide the most reliable information. Blindly following the expert opinion can and more often than we realize, will lead you astray.

Concerning finances, the 1% simply have more and better information. The first six chapters of this book were written in January and February of 2020, and during that time, we were in the longest economic expansion in our Nation's history. In those first chapters, I wrote a lot about stocks, my parents, retirement, and the market eventually crashing. I had no idea that the market would crash before this book would be published. It is happening now though, in the middle of writing this book. It is now May of 2020, and we are living through unprecedented unemployment, and some of the largest stock drops since the great depression.

Economically, things are grim, and even worse, the health and lives of the people we love are at stake. It's a perfect storm, and I'd be lying if I told you that I wasn't concerned.

However, when I think about 9/11, I realize that I've been through some of this before. After 9/11, business literally stopped. We were scared about future terrorists; we were scared that the economy would never recover: we were simply scared. The crux of fear lies in uncertainty, and Wall Street hates uncertainty. It's melting down, but it will rise again. I'm sure of it.

The virus, and this broader 2020 meltdown, is a surprise and a shock. The financial collapse is not, because we knew that it was going to happen. Maybe not as dramatically as it's happening now, but we knew it would happen eventually nonetheless. What is also a fact is that the market will recover, and the market will come back stronger than before. It is only a matter of time. But, just as we didn't know when it was going to crash, we don't know when it is going to recover, either. Just like the experts said that the air was safe at ground zero, I don't know, you don't know, and the "experts" certainly don't know how this whole thing is going to play out both economically and from a health perspective. Yet we listen to them. Even after everything I know, I often listen to them too. It's so very hard to change that wiring I grew up with, and especially in times of fear I fall back into those old patterns of thinking. The difference today, though, is I'm aware when I do, and can most of the time get back on course before I make many serious mistakes.

I want to share a true story, and my financial advisor, who is a wonderful and very intelligent man, will back me up on this. In early February this year, I was on a flight from New York to Dulles, VA, and I sat next to a gentleman who was on his way to Washington to participate in a Coronavirus task force. The Coronavirus had a solid foothold in China at that time, and we were concerned that it was going to come to the United States. My seatmate shared some of his opinions with me on that flight, and, when I landed at Dulles, I called my advisor and told him that I thought it was time to move even more money out of the market. I asked him to find what I could sell while paying the least amount of tax on the profits. He graciously did an analysis for me, and we found out that it would have cost me a fortune in taxes to move that money out.

Ultimately, I decided the money I had in stocks wouldn't be needed for ten years or so, if ever, and told him to just leave it in. Next, I called my husband and recapped the conversation I had just with the man on the plane, and told him I thought it was time he moved some of his retirement money out of the market. Over the next several days I spoke with some of my Wall Street friends, medical friends, and my family. Most thought I was overreacting. Many of my friends, and my spouse, thought I was crazy when I told them what the man on that 45-minute flight had shared with me. My point is, after speaking with the smartest finance people I knew, getting the opinion of my family and closest friends, and reading what I could on how the experts thought that the coronavirus would impact the markets, the advice I ultimately should have acted on was the advice that I got from a completely random stranger on a plane.

Even more interesting is how I was well into writing this book at the time of the coronavirus economic disaster. I knew about the high costs of mutual funds, and how we are programmed and hard-wired to think about money. I knew about all of those things. I also knew about hidden investments that were much less volatile than the public markets. I knew all of this, and I still didn't act. I trusted my wiring instead. I trusted 40 years of conventional wisdom, instead of what I've come to believe about that conventional wisdom.

Over the last couple of months I've been on the phone with my fellow real estate investors. I told them to remain calm, and know that the universe expands. This is all going to be okay, and the most important thing is to focus on staying healthy at this juncture. The market will roar back stronger than ever, and from this crisis, new opportunities that we could never have imagined will emerge. Just like the tragedy and heartbreak of 9/11 was followed by new opportunities and abundance, just like the financial crisis of 2008 saw the economy come back even stronger than before, the COVID-19 pandemic will be the same.

Here's what you may not realize, though. I'm confident that the 1% is already bouncing back. It is 9AM, and the market is going to open soon. I've had CNBC on over the past two hours, and the DJIA futures have gone from +110 to +720, and now it is at +121. Why? Because Wall Street is buying and selling, while we have no idea what we should do, and many of us are still asleep. They are making money 24/7, whether the market goes up or down.

One of the things that I have loved about living in NYC for the past 30 years is that I've been able to get to know some incredibly interesting and intelligent people, from all over the world, and who grew up very, very differently than I did. I knew about Wall Street, but I had actually never met anyone who worked there. As a matter of fact, I am honestly not sure I even knew that Wall Street was a real place in NYC. Either way, I now know plenty of Wall Street executives and call them my friends. Bond traders, investment bankers, stockbrokers, analysts, hedge fund managers—you name it. I knew that most of them worked a lot of hours, and I knew that they made a lot of money. Silly me thought that they were making $1M, $2M, or maybe even $3M annually. Nope. Not everyone, (I want to stress that), but many of the top are making more, sometimes significantly more than that.

According to a survey conducted by *Institutional Investor magazine*, the average US-based hedge fund manager expected to bring home around $1.4M in 2018. The very top hedge fund managers can make much, much more, and the top 3 or 4 of them made close to $1B that year. The top mutual fund managers can make several million dollars annually. Granted, these are senior-level people, and there are plenty of people that make far less than that, but there are a whole lot of people that work in the financial services industry that make a ton of money.

I'm not opposed to anyone making money, however, the amazing thing to me is the fact that Wall

Street makes money whether you and I make money or not. They may make more if you make money, but they get paid handsomely whether you make money or not.

While the public markets are going down, those who have a net worth high enough to meet the minimum investment amount for participation in institutional private funds, and those who simply know about hidden investments, are investing like crazy. This is a fantastic time for those who have the resources that are large enough to make trades that are capable of moving the market. Ultra-high net worth typically comes with advisors who have the skills, tools, and know the inner workings of the stock market and our tax code. Unless we know they exist and we look for them, simply the mere existence of those private funds, financial products, and the advisors are hidden from the rest of us. While publicly traded stocks crash, private money is often capitalizing on that downturn. The "experts" simply report on what those market makers are doing. By the time we hear about it, the big money has usually already been made.

CHAPTER 8:
Myth #8
Hire A Financial Advisor To Plan Your Retirement

Reality: You are smarter than you think. Most financial advisors don't have access to better information than you do.

Prior to online trading, individual investors had very little direct access to the market to buy stocks or funds. Instead, they placed their orders through a licensed broker, usually by phone. These brokers knew the leverage they commanded and charged high commissions without consequence. Today, most people execute trades via online brokerages and pay relatively very little in the way of transaction fees. Retail brokers may still execute orders, but most have expanded their services to include investment management, and most of them today call themselves Financial Advisors.

Here in the United States, Financial Advisers are held to scrupulous legal standards. As I mentioned in an earlier chapter, investment advisers must adhere to the Investment Advisers Act of 1940, which requires them to perform fiduciary duties in regards to any investment products they recommend to their clients. The law states that an advisor has, "An obligation not to subordinate the clients' interests to its own."

That said, a financial advisor may only be able to recommend products and services that they have access to. Your 401K is like a walled garden with a finite number of investment choices, and some of the better options lay just outside those walls. Financial advisors often work for large firms, and what they recommend usually closely aligns with the values of said firm.

I want to be perfectly clear that I have a financial advisor myself, and I think he's fantastic. He is very smart, and a good friend who I totally believe wants the best for me. I honestly feel guilty almost every time I talk to him these days, because more times than not, I end up moving more money out of my investment accounts. I pay him 1% of the value of all of my accounts, so when I move money he loses money! I don't fault anyone for making money, and he provides an important service. I know that he's managing carefully and earning competitive returns, but he is limited by the system he works within.

Through him I am invested in an assortment of mutual funds that, for the most part have made money, but have not been tax-friendly at all. At this point in my investing journey, I am simply not making enough return on investment to justify the fees and taxes, especially when I begin comparing those returns to some of my other, more profitable investments.

However, I didn't have a ton of investing experience when I first got started with my advisor. Like many people, I found him because his partner was the father of a friend. He and his partner are great people and very smart. At the time, I was busy with my career and launching my life, and honestly, having someone to hold my hand and pay close attention to my investments was well worth the fees. Of course, now I know that I was paying far more in hidden mutual fund fees.

But at that stage of my life, having a professional help manage my investments made sense.

Regardless of whether the investment firm is large or small, most financial advisors do indeed charge around 1 percent of your portfolio, and that is in addition to all of the fees that we discussed in prior chapters of this book. That means that before you even begin building wealth, your portfolio is GUARANTEED to underperform the market by 1 percent. Why? Most financial advisors, in fact, almost all of them, don't outperform the market.

In a previous chapter, we compared a managed fund with the natural growth of the stock market and found the two to be effectively identical. Not only that, but the fees themselves cut into your gains. By the time you see the returns, the parent investment company, the fund manager, the brokers trading within the fund, the retail broker, and then finally your financial advisor, have all taken their cut. I saw this firsthand when I was paying fees and taxes in astronomical figures. I saw my savings being slowly chipped away by private companies and the government.

In short, each mutual fund has a fund manager that I'm paying to watch my portfolio. I'm paying for all of the administrative expenses that the mutual funds incur, as well as the fees that they charge my financial advisor for the privilege and support of being able to offer them. Then I pay fees to my financial advisor, and then taxes on top of the whole thing. Sounds crazy when you see it all spelled out in one place doesn't it?

Today, I understand how it really works. I've learned the secrets to higher revenue streams and fewer fees and taxes. Even knowing all of that, I think so highly of my advisor that I probably will wait to take all of my money out. However, the majority of my net worth is no longer in publicly-traded securities.

There is no end to the books and articles that are readily available for you to learn more about financial planners. At the end of the day, all of us don't know exactly what they don't know. Just as most of us are hard-wired from a young age to think that we need to hire a financial planner and let him or her manage our money, financial planners suffer from the same failings. They went to the same schools as the rest of us, and they consume the same media that we do. After they finished college, most went to work for a financial services company that taught them all about the products they offer and how to present them to their clients. As their career progressed, they learned more and more about what their employers wanted them to know. So much of what they learn is given to them by the companies they represent, and those companies, at the end of the day, are profit-driven. They want to give you enough of a return that you don't walk across the street to their competitor while maintaining their own profit margins. I get it, and they provide a valuable service to many people. Just be aware of the bigger picture.

Some financial opportunities are hidden from us. Those in the top 1 percent of net worth have access to hidden investments, as well as accountants and lawyers who are putting deals together before they are offered, if at all, to the rest of us. Most advisors to the wealthy have an intimate knowledge of our tax code, understand how investments and our tax code go hand in hand, and take full advantage of the laws of our land.

Professional investors like Warren Buffet or Carl Icahn might buy stock on the open market, but they buy tens-of-millions in shares. Shares of this quantity can give them a voice in the management of the company. If they have a large enough interest in the company, they might increase dividends, or sell assets to benefit other businesses that they own. If you have enough control, there is no limit in potential opportunities. Additionally, when you buy that much stock in one company, the stock usually goes up, offering an option to sell quickly for a fast return. Their investments literally move the needle. The market can be manipulated once you start working with large enough figures. The richest in the world can influence and therefore capitalize on the markets in a way that the rest of us simply cannot do with our limited investments.

By doing this, the richest can earn a better return than the overall stock market, but they're not really "beating the market." Instead, they're just manipulating the specifics of business for their own ends. Large investment banks do the same thing, using the money from private funds from their ultra-high net worth clients. Unless you have a net worth large enough to play, the public equity markets will always leave the leftovers to the average investor. We think that those leftovers are good because that's what we've been told our entire lives. In reality it can be, but most of the time it's the luck of the draw for us. For the Uber-Wealthy, the risks can be mitigated and the returns can balloon well beyond what you or I would ever be capable of.

A study of the ultra-wealthy by the private equity firm KKR found that the ultra-wealthy certainly hold equities, but that an average of 31 percent of them are public. The other 59 percent of them are hidden from the rest of us, consisting primarily of hedge funds, private equity, and real assets such as real estate, art, and precious metals. The KKR study also showed that the ultra-wealthy were consistently early to embrace capital markets' dislocation. This meant that during periodic market shocks, such as the Chinese currency devaluation, the rich were spending capital while everyone else was holding on to their savings or pulling out. The study also noted that these wealthy clients would move quickly to take advantage of shifting laws and regulations. Whenever a favorable investment emerges, the richest move billions of dollars to maximize returns. The wealthiest citizens continually profit off of market volatility with this investment edge.

In short, the top 1 percent, and especially the top .5%, have the net worth that is required to invest with the top private equity and hedge funds and take advantage of their intimate knowledge of hidden investments, exploit their influence, and reap returns that aren't available to the rest of us.

However, until the last decade or so because so much more information is available, the laws began to change. Entrepreneurs like me and my partners are now able to purchase cash-flowing real estate assets from many of those private funds, offering them directly to private, mostly-accredited investors, like you and me. A good private real estate syndication or any other good hidden investment will pay investors first, as opposed to investors making what is left after everyone gets their piece of the action. I know that to be especially true in most of the multifamily syndications that I invest in.

Now that you know that there is even a thing called multifamily syndication, you only have to use any search engine or go to my website www.keepmore.com, to find out more. Remember though, things may sound scary, too good to be true, and will most likely conflict with your hard-wired beliefs. Keep an open mind. You might just change the way you think about investing and planning for your retirement.

CHAPTER 9:

Myth #9

Real Estate Investing Is Risky And Unpredictable

Reality: Cash-Flowing Real Estate is one of the safest and stable investments available if you understand how to mitigate risk.

Cash Flow or Appreciation?

Perhaps the most common myth I hear when discussing investing is that real estate can be very risky.

That is true in many cases, and like anything else, if you don't know what to look for and understand the risks, it's not hard to lose money. But what many don't understand is that just as with any investment, you need to have a primary goal for that investment. With real estate, as well as most other investments, the first thing you need to decide is whether or not you want to invest for cash flow or invest for appreciation.

Many people, especially those who live in places like New York and California, don't understand. In New York City, it's almost impossible to buy anything when cash flow is the primary objective. In NY, it's all about buying something and holding onto it while the market appreciates. What's the biggest risk? The market may go down, just as it has as I write this book. Real estate in NYC has plummeted, while real estate outside of the city and in other parts of the country is doing much, much better. With COVID-19, fewer people want to live in big cities right now, and who can blame them? Who knows when we will feel comfortable going out like we used to, so making sure that your investments are cash flowing. Planning for the worst-case scenario is the way I want to invest—period.

Because our brains are wired to think of investing as buying something now, such as a stock, and wait for it to go up, people think of real estate investing the same way because that's how their brain works. However, in many parts of the country, it is possible to buy real estate that turns a profit immediately. Cash flowing real estate means that after all of the expenses, including taxes, property management, maintenance, and any other operating expenses, are paid, there is money left over after rents are collected.

When I say cash-flowing real estate, I mean that it is self-sustaining and making money even before I buy it. As a matter of fact, I want rents to be able to drop 25% at a minimum before I lose money. The chances of finding a deal like that in NYC, LA, or SF are fairly slim, but people do it every day in states such as Texas, the Carolinas, and Florida.

It's possible with single-family homes in many markets as well, but it's tough to find a house that cash-flows very much at the end of the day. However, tenants can pay the mortgage and if the rent will cover the expenses, you eventually own the home. To really plan a retirement around that strategy if the houses have mortgages on them, it would take multiple houses and that becomes very hard to scale.

However, let's say you buy a 100-500-unit apartment complex where each unit is cash flowing even $300 each month. Now your cash flow is $30K-$150K monthly, it's a relatively small area so logistics are easier than driving all around town, you can buy 100s of stoves when it's time to replace them…you get the idea.

Assuming the asset is cash-flowing today, if we buy it with 30% down and plan for rents to drop if there is a recession, we can mitigate much of the risk and my dependence on the role that outside market forces play in my future goes down exponentially.

My friend Joe Fairless talks about the three immutable laws of real estate investing that, when followed, can enable real estate investors to thrive in any market, at any time in the market cycle. Since 2014, when markets were appreciating everywhere, I stayed the course and paid attention to Joe's three laws. I believe he's right, so I want to make sure that I take the time to share all three with you:

1) Buy for cash flow

2) Secure long-term, low leveraged debt

3) Have adequate cash reserves.

Law #1 – Buy for Cash Flow

The opposite of buying for cash flow is buying for appreciation. And in particular, organic market appreciation. As we clearly see with the stock market, what happens organically in the marketplace is completely out of our control.

When you buy for cash flow, you will care far less about what the market is doing. In fact, if the market takes a dip, the demand for rentals will likely increase, even in the middle of a pandemic, a fact we are seeing in most of our properties right now.

Law #2 – Secure Long-Term, Low Leveraged Debt

The leverage that comes from financing is one of the main benefits of investing in real estate. Let's say you have $100,000 to invest. If you decide to invest all of that money into a stock, you would control $100,000 worth of that stock. On the other hand, if you wanted to invest all of that money in real estate, you could spend $100,000 on a down payment at 80% loan-to-value and control $500,000 worth of real estate. That's the power of leverage from financing.

But there's also a catch. With leverage comes a mortgage, which you must continue to pay each month. If you fail to make a payment or cannot sell/refinance once the loan comes due, the bank will take the property.

The less money put into a deal—or more specifically, the less equity you have in a deal—the more over-leveraged you are. Consequently, the higher your mortgage payments will be. In a hot market, over-leveraging may seem like a brilliant idea, but what happens when property value or rental rates start to drop?

Well, if you purchase a property with less than 20% down and the market drops by 5%, 10% or 20% (which has happened in the past) by the end of your loan term, you are forced to sell the property at a lower than projected price (maybe even at a loss) or you are forced to give the property back to the bank. You should have a bare minimum of 20% equity going into a deal, and a loan that covers 2x the length of your business plan/how long you plan to keep the property.

You will almost always be able to secure a loan with a term that is shorter than your business plan and with less than 20% equity, that's how many people get into trouble. Securing long-term, low leveraged debt, in tandem with committing to buy for cash flow, will allow you to continue covering your mortgage payments and avoid having negative equity in the event of a downturn.

Law #3 – Have Adequate Cash Reserves

When you don't have adequate cash reserves, you won't have funds to cover an unexpected expense. I like to have 1-5% of the purchase price in operating reserves at all times.

Don't buy for appreciation, don't over-leverage and don't get forced to sell when you aren't ready to. This is all easier said than done, and I found that real estate investing on my own was more work than I had time for.

Then I found multifamily syndication.

CHAPTER 10:

Myth #10

The Good Deals In Real Estate Are All Gone

Reality: There are more checks and balances than you think, and the A-list syndicators are accessible if you know where to look. Once you build a few relationships, doors will open.

Because real estate is tax-friendly, simple to understand, and probably the most steady and conservative investment out there, I've worked to learn as much as I can about the industry. My experience has consistently shown that a private multifamily syndication specifically is the best way for any working professional to invest in real estate. Here's why this particular investment route can be so appealing:

First and foremost, it's truly passive. It is possible to enjoy almost all the benefits of real estate investing without having to source the deal, get the loan, close on the property, manage the property, deal with tenants, and all the other legwork it takes to get a deal off the ground. You don't have time for that. In a syndication, someone else does all the work, and you reap the benefits.

Secondly, a multifamily syndication is an EQUITY investment. You are buying real estate along with many others. They are a safe and steady place to invest to diversify from the stock market, and you can start with as little as $50,000.

Unlike other investments, multifamily syndications offer a steady cash flow with unbelievable tax benefits.

And the investors come first. Period. Investors get paid first, and there are no huge fees or hidden charges. That money goes to you instead.

Multifamily syndication opportunities can appear complicated and obscure at first. People are afraid of the commitment and the perceived lack of control that they have. In reality, multifamily syndications are significantly less complicated than investing in a mutual fund, because a mutual fund typically lacks 100% alignment of interest.

Most mutual fund managers get paid whether the fund makes money or not. Granted they will make MORE money the better it performs, but they will still make a very good living. Call or write to your mutual fund company and ask for a FULL (not a summary) prospectus and you will see what I mean. It's scary stuff.

One of the biggest concerns in new investors is what to look for when searching for these investment opportunities. You can find out a lot more by visiting my website, www.hiddeninvesting.com, but I want to first share five important elements that I familiarize myself with fully before making any investment.

These five are: The team, the business plan, the asset, the market and submarket, and the fees and distributions. These five pieces together will almost guarantee a successful and steadily profitable investment.

The Team

As a Limited Partner, you must fully trust your General Partner team. They control the P&L, and they are responsible for every major decision in the project, from finding the deals and financing, to actively managing and working with investors. The project lives and dies with the leadership of your General Partners. Therefore, it is crucial that you do your research ahead of time. Get to know them, and make sure you are confident in their ability before putting your money in their hands.

Running an apartment community is a business. How much business experience do they have? How long have they been in multifamily, and what have their successes and failures looked like? Do they have a team of underwriters, property managers, and brokers with real multifamily experience? More importantly, are they also investing capital? How much personal stake does each carry in the project? Any good syndicator should be able to answer all of those questions on the spot. Additionally, anyone that you invest with should be more than willing to provide references and agree to a background check. If they are concerned about either of those things, run away fast.

Do investors get paid before anyone else? Syndications should be structured with investors as the priority. Typically, there is a preferred return that investors get paid first, and then any management compensation is directly tied to the performance of the asset.

Being a Limited Partner, you should be paid preferred returns before anyone else, and the distribution of those returns should be in favor of the investor. That split typically starts around 70/30, in favor of the limited partners, and then as certain predetermined hurdles are achieved that changes as those are passed. General Partners themselves, as individuals, should be investing alongside you as well.

The Business Plan

The business plan should first make sense. It is the foundation of the project, and it must be airtight before any other moves can be made. Ask yourself, "Are the goals and timeline of this project clearly vetted and outlined? My team prioritizes cash flow and capital preservation. We go in and make enhancements to the property, and add management efficiencies to increase the net operating income, hence the value. All of those plans must make sense.

Any project needs to have secure long-term financing, at a minimum covering twice the time that the business plan outlines. They also require a reserve fund for unforeseen expenses, and well-researched underwriting assumptions put in place to weather the fallout of a down-cycle market. Decisions like rent increase need to be realistic and grounded in the surrounding markets.

You should also be asking, "Is the projected growth realistic and sustainable? "When do the investors start seeing returns? What does the exit strategy look like, what the risks are, and exactly what the partners plan to do to mitigate those risks? All of those things should be well-established and clearly articulated.

The Market and Submarket

The market should have diverse job opportunities, not tied to one or two particular industries. This is often the biggest pitfall for new investors. They find a perfect investment opportunity with an amazing property, but it's in a market composed of over 50% military, or the automotive industry, or oil and gas, etc. Dallas is a market that I've worked in extensively, and companies like Toyota, McKesson, United Scientific Group, Fluor, and over 1500 others, call the DFW Metro Area home.

What are the demographic trends of the area? Are those static or changing? Is the population growing or declining? What does the surrounding area look like? Are there new local businesses emerging? What does transportation look like?

Another aspect that new investors often overlook is how "Investor-Friendly" the city, state, or regions is. This is somewhat subjective, but generally states like Texas and Florida are very landlord-friendly. New York and similar states have all kinds of laws and regulations that favor the tenants. This doesn't rule them out as potential investments, but it adds another factor to consider when looking for investment opportunities.

Thousands of garden-style multifamily properties are located throughout the United States. Since they aren't building more of them, and most target the "working American" demographic, I like those in particular. Most people, even those who live and work there, don't know who actually owns them. They are owned by hedge funds, REITs, wealthy families, and people like you and me.

Mitigation of Risk In the Event of a Downturn

In the back of your mind you may be wondering what happens to a Real Estate investment in the event of a market crash. The 2008 financial crisis still sits in the back of everyone's mind, and the prospect of sinking capital into a long-term project can feel daunting. Today's market can feel even more daunting.

The good news is that apartment syndication as an investment is significantly safer than the stock market.

As an investor, I try to diversify my portfolio, and stocks are one such option. But I would strongly recommend not putting all of your savings into stocks or any other single investment category.

Let's use that 2008 collapse as an example to highlight the difference between the two investment options.

When the markets collapsed, the housing prices tanked. The rent prices however, barely moved. In high-growth areas where my company invests, a 2016 US Census American Community Survey study showed that rent prices moved as little as 10 percent during the downturn. Rent is one of the few areas that remain mostly unaffected by an economic downturn. Furthermore, with a default rate of only 0.4 percent, multifamily assets had one of the lowest default rates nationwide with only a 0.4% default rate. Even today, in most markets tenants are paying their rent during this pandemic. In markets like NYC, people are being told that they don't need to pay their rents, some aren't, but most are. Our properties are certainly working with tenants, and our tenants appreciate that. Remember, we work hard to provide nice places for everyone to live. Everyone is working together to get through this together.

It is precisely because of this fact that multifamily syndications are typically safe and steady. Everyone needs a place to live. That will always be the case. And in recessions, fewer people are buying and more people are renting. Oftentimes, high-end renters will live below their means and trade down. That upper group provides a new stream of tenants who want affordable but comfortable living. That's where we come in. My company prioritizes class B properties—the kind that remains mostly stable and in high demand in most markets in the country.

The Real Estate market will go up and down. That cycle always repeats itself, but if you focus on mitigating risk, you will be much more prepared for the inevitable downturn.

Here's what I specifically recommend to mitigate risk:

Most importantly, never buy for appreciation. Buy for cash flow. This guarantees that you can hold onto the asset as needed until the market improves without fear of having a massive money-suck draining your reserves.

Secure long-term financing if possible. This ensures you won't be forced to sell the asset before you can start turning a profit. These types of loans are becoming more difficult to secure, but a strong team with solid relationships and an established history will go a long way towards negotiating a fair deal.

Another point is to always buy in a growing market. Texas and the Carolinas are two of the hottest areas in the country, but there are smaller cities all around the U.S. that still have a real need for housing.

Always think about the worst-case scenario. Plan conservatively and you'll never be caught off guard when things go south. When the economy does crash however, the stock market is going to crash first. No matter what happens, apartment communities can offer steady income and a stable investment in a way stocks will never be able to.

I strongly believe that every investor should have a multifamily investment in their portfolio. Their safety and consistency truly make them a step above every other investment option in times of crisis.

My Real Life Example

I want to use a real-life asset I've acquired to show you an example of what I'm talking about. We acquired an asset just out of Charlotte NC earlier this month. In the deal we set aside just over 1.2 million in operating reserves, and we set a conservative, 55 percent break-even occupancy rate. This would mean just under half of the building could be empty and we would still be able to pay debts and expenses.

The property has been in operation since 2014 and the occupancy is at 96 percent, and has never dropped below 90 percent. This allows a lot of breathing room and ensures that the property is cash-flowing from day one. We plan to secure a 10-year, low-interest agency debt to shield us from market volatility.

The submarket that it's located in has seen steady population growth through the past five years and is projected to only get larger through 2024. These are the types of investments we seek out. We are confident the asset can and will continue to provide passive steady revenue for the next decade.

My income is going up, and my daughter will be able to keep the principal and all the assets when I'm gone. Contrast that with what happened to my parents, and keeping you from that is why I wrote this book.

We can all do this. We all have the potential to invest and start growing our generational wealth. This has been around a long time. It's just been hidden. My goal is for you to have your eyes open and start exploring things with an open mind as I did because it can change your life.

Conclusion

Ultimately, it is up to you how you invest your hard-earned money. Your own financial goals will dictate whether a particular opportunity is right for you.

After I had accumulated a few passive real estate investments and learned more about the industry, I organically began to meet other investors. Through those contacts, I've learned about and invested in many other private opportunities, such as self-storage and mortgage notes. I intend to write a second book later this year and focus on other hidden, alternative investments that are available beyond Wall Street. Countless opportunities sit just out of reach of the public.

The release of this book is happening at an unprecedented time in our history. COVID-19 is scary and is impacting our lives in dramatic ways. No one is escaping this pandemic unscathed, but I know that we will get through this and emerge stronger than ever. No one knows what will happen in the coming months, but as I sit here today with more people out of work, and stocks lower than we could have imagined, I will tell you that most of my multifamily syndications are still cash-flowing just as they were before. I'm grateful for that.

We didn't plan for a global pandemic, but we did plan on a severe economic downturn. My greatest joy this month has been to watch my friends see the power of alternative investing firsthand, and the security that investments backed by hard assets can offer.

I don't know when this will end or what will happen, other than it will end someday, and we will be stronger because of it. The economy will come back, and our country will soar to ever-greater heights. I will tell you though, that I am also SURE that after that next period of amazing prosperity, there will be another economic downturn. I don't know when and I don't know how, but I know that it will happen. We need to change our thinking, and look beyond what everyone else is doing. You must be prepared. I hope that this book has given you a view into how the wealthy emerge time and time again from these events relatively unscathed, and how you can too.

We have reached the end of our journey together. Moving forward, if you so wish, a great way to connect with me personally is the HiddenInvesting Facebook group. On top of it being the perfect place to meet other like-minded investors, we share resources and other valuable information on a weekly basis. My websites, hiddeninvesting.com, and keepmore.com are similarly useful places to do some additional research and learn more about multifamily syndications.

Conclusion

No matter what you do, all the best for your continued health and happiness, and I'm grateful that you've come this far with me.

Endnotes

1. "Real Estate Investment Trusts (REITs)." Real Estate Investment Trusts (REITs) | Investor.gov, www.investor.gov/introduction-investing/investing-basics/investment-products/real-estate-investment-trusts-reits.

2. Smith, Liz. "401(k) Fees: Everything You Need to Know." SmartAsset, SmartAsset, 12 Dec. 2019, smartasset.com/retirement/what-are-401k-fees.

3. Employee Benefits Security Administration, US Department of Labor. "A Look At 401K Fees." U.S. Department of Labor, Employee Benefits Security Administration (EBSA), U.S. Department of Labor, Employee Benefits Security Administration (EBSA), 2019, U.S. Department of Labor, Employee Benefits Security Administration (EBSA).

4. Inc., Morningstar. "Morningstar, Inc." Morningstar, 2020, www.morningstar.com/markets?CustId=&CLogin=&CType=&CName=&_LPAGE=%2FFORBIDDEN%2FCONTENTARCHIVED.HTML&_BPA=N.

5. Harper, David R. "Hedge Funds: Higher Returns Or Just High Fees?" Investopedia, Investopedia, 29 May 2020, www.investopedia.com/articles/03/121003.asp.

Made in the USA
Columbia, SC
12 August 2020